PRAISE FOR JACKIE BARRETT AND
THE DEVIL I KNOW

"If this is the final word on the matter straight from the killer's mouth, it has ended the only way it could have. Barrett has given us one last look at the case that engulfed New York, and does not disappoint."

—*Fangoria Magazine*

"Jaw-dropping, utterly fascinating." —*Mobile Ghosts*

"Barrett is a wonderful writer and the details . . . about the Amityville case that come to light through her interactions with DeFeo are fascinating . . . Barrett does give readers an intimate look into the mind of a notorious killer and an in-depth description of what she has experienced as someone with extraordinary gifts." —*Library of the Dead*

"Fans of horror and of true crime are certain to enjoy this book . . . [*The Devil I Know*] is a book you must add to your . . . reading list. Highly recommended."

—*Jenn's Bookshelves*

Berkley titles by Jackie Barrett

THE DEVIL I KNOW

THE HAUNTING OF THE GEMINI

THE
HAUNTING
OF THE
GEMINI

A True Story of New York's Zodiac Murders

JACKIE BARRETT

BERKLEY BOOKS, NEW YORK

THE BERKLEY PUBLISHING GROUP
Published by the Penguin Group
Penguin Group (USA) LLC
375 Hudson Street, New York, New York 10014

USA • Canada • UK • Ireland • Australia • New Zealand • India • South Africa • China

penguin.com

A Penguin Random House Company

THE HAUNTING OF THE GEMINI

A Berkley Book / published by arrangement with the author

For information, address: The Berkley Publishing Group,
a division of Penguin Group (USA) LLC,
375 Hudson Street, New York, New York 10014.

ISBN: 978-0-425-26722-6

PUBLISHING HISTORY
Berkley premium edition / March 2014

PRINTED IN THE UNITED STATES OF AMERICA

10 9 8 7 6 5 4 3 2 1

Cover art: *Skyline of downtown New York* © beboy/Shutterstock;
Zodiac signs © Svitlana Amelina/Shutterstock.
Cover design by Jane Hammer.

For William, Joanne, Jude, and Jane.

In loving memory of Patricia Fonti, 1953–1992.
You will never be forgotten.
Out of this world and into the next.
Lost, but found.

ACKNOWLEDGMENTS

I would like to thank Claire Booth, an award-winning journalist who was able to dive deep into my world of the notorious and sinister minds and souls on this side and in the afterlife. Some bonds will never be broken, as some paths are meant to cross. Your exceptional dedication and wittiness shines through. My gratitude you have.

I would also like to thank Shannon Jamieson Vazquez, my brilliant editor at Berkley Books, who takes pride in detail and has a truly extraordinary perception of true crime, life and death, heaven and hell. My deepest respect you shall always have.

Jim McCarthy, my agent and vice president of Dystel and Goderich Literary Management, is an incredible man of leadership and knowledge. I'm proud to call you my friend. Never lose your humor!

To my husband, William, words cannot express my love for you. Into my many shades of darkness, you shined light. Your patience and strength are remarkable. You have been my hero, never being too far behind me. Loving you now and ever after.

My talented and amazing daughter, Joanne Agnelli, is also my partner and executive assistant. There isn't a person alive who could fill your shoes. Your magical energy has healed and touched countless souls, including my own. I'm blessed to have such a relationship. Loving you.

I also want to express my appreciation to retired police captain Sean Crowley, who has never left my side, even when I disappeared into the seedier side of life and death. You are my forever partner and kin. You're incredible.

And I could never forget to thank Jude Weng, who holds so many titles—executive producer, director, writer, negotiator. You always put my best interests first and are one of the few who knows the many sides of Jackie. You are a true believer who has traveled many journeys and encouraged me to challenge the two tigers that reside within me. One is fear, and the other is courage. You touched my life, and I am forever grateful!

And last, to my two Maltese puppies, Teddy and Miss Violet, who showed me that I could love again. The proof and power of love comes in many forms. Meeting up with two old souls isn't so unusual for me, whether they have two legs or four. Love never dies.

Twinkle, twinkle, little star
How I wonder who you are
In the dark, you stalked the night
With your mask, holding a knife

—JACKIE BARRETT

PROLOGUE

There had been many doors, many different choices he could have made. But he had seen only one. He knew what was behind it, and he opened it anyway. And so the devil came to stay.

When he was a child, he would kill animals with little homemade bombs, or torture them with fire. He was very interested in their screams. In school, he would daydream. The walls would change color to a murky dark green, and blood would drip down the walls. Everyone else would be dead in their seats. Pools of blood from slashed throats covered the desks. The room would be still and silent.

He was in high school when he first began to plan. He brought a homemade gun to school and got caught and thrown out. He was rejected by the army after failing its tests, and his frustration grew. He went to peep shows to see all those dirty, rotten whores shaking their asses for a dollar in quarters. He liked to look, not touch. It felt good to be an intruder. He could violate every inch without being seen. He could have easily approached any one of those women, said a few nice things, gone back to her place, and had sex. But that wasn't what he wanted. He didn't need what was between his legs. Just what flowed in their veins. The feeling of shooting or slicing someone was what made his body shake.

He would lock himself in his room at home, making his own bullets and assembling his own guns. He couldn't even write properly, yet he began to understand certain codes and hieroglyphics, symbols and signs, other components of the occult. He had not studied to earn this knowledge, but it was suddenly there, helping him get closer to fulfilling his needs.

He didn't need food or water. He didn't get hungry. He was just empty, except for the hate, the anger, and the lust. When he looked in the mirror, he saw that his pupils had vanished. All that remained were two all-black eyes. The day he first signed his mark, he felt like he was two people in one body. One hand did not belong to him. It was as if he had a twin. That other hand was not his conscience, though. He didn't have one.

As he roamed the dark streets night after night, he started to notice the stench. He had always been clean, always hated dirt and dirty people. But now, no matter how often he showered, he stank of rotting meat. His breath smelled like shit, and the odor of a slaughterhouse seemed to ooze from every pore. He knew—the more he became the beast, the more he smelled like one.

Before he would go out, before he would kill, he needed to get ready. So he would stand in his tiny childhood room and put on the mask. This was his own private one, not the bandanna he wore out to hunt. It was a ski hat with holes cut into it for his eyes and nose. He would pull it over his face when he conducted his rituals, when he wrote the symbols and spoke the words that summoned the dark gods. He pulled on his second skin and became the devil.

He always wrote the letters first. He knew what their signs were before he shot them. So he wrote the notes that included the signs of his victims and left them near the scenes of his shootings. The devil always knows a person's sign. And so he did, too.

The devil helped in other ways as well. The one victim who'd been able to give the cops a description had gotten it all wrong. The pigs were searching for someone who looked nothing like him—a man who was even of a different race. That proved very helpful as he continued to do his work. Even the prostitutes he would see at the park could never remember his face. It was as if he were invisible, which was of great benefit when you had so much work to do. He still had not found that special someone—his perfect victim. He had to keep looking.

He would stand before the mirror with his face covered and slowly glide a knife over his body, touching his nipples with its tip. He would lean forward, closer to his reflection. "You want me to fuck you? Come closer, let me smell you. Whore . . ." The knife would go between his legs until he came in his own tight black pants, turning them sticky until they dried to his flesh. He did this for himself because no one else was worthy of touching him.

He would pull on his heavy black boots and arm himself.

He placed a gun in the back of his waistband and one down his boot. He saved a special makeshift gun for the front, shoving it down in his pants so that it touched his penis. The cold metal and the thought of using it made him hard.

He would twist and turn as candles illuminated his moving reflection. Sweat formed on his brow, and his eyes darkened. He reached for a small bowl of water soaked with oils and herbs that sat next to his ritual book, which contained information about the Seal of Solomon, an ancient talisman of great power. He had no intention of using that knowledge for good but instead wanted it to help increase his own power and to blind others to his presence and the unholy acts he longed to commit. His hands dipped into the liquid and brought it to the mask, where he anointed himself by trickling drops into his eyes and mouth. The mask absorbed the rest and, with it, the last remnants of his humanity. One last stare deep into the mirror, and the Zodiac was ready.

ONE

———

When I was eight years old, I died. I died on the operating table as doctors tried to take out my appendix. It had ruptured, and the contamination caused me to go into shock. I flatlined for more than three minutes. A large and immediate blood transfusion was the only thing that brought me back, the doctors said.

But they hadn't gone where I had. They hadn't followed me into the bright tunnel. Yes, it was indeed a tunnel, where I felt happy and weightless. A dog came running toward me, barking cheerfully, and he was followed by my grandfather—my father's father, a Native American medicine man who had passed away years before. I ran forward and hugged him. He reached up and took a medicine bag from around his neck and put it around mine.

The tunnel began to fill with people, standing behind my grandfather and blocking the way through to the other side. One appeared off to the side, a very tall man dressed in black. My grandfather bent down toward me. "You must fight this man," he said, as the man began walking toward me. "You must go back and follow your spirit. Never forget who you are." Then he turned around and walked away from me, fading away, along with the protective crowd of people. "You shall win," he said as he vanished, leaving me alone with the tall man in black.

I wanted desperately to run after my grandfather, but I couldn't move. The tall man took my hand and grinned at me. "Jackie, you'll grow to realize that things are already set. If I let you go now, it will change everything else." He turned me back the way I'd come. I tried to resist. "Cheer up," he said. "I thought you would like a good fight. I will watch you as you watch me, and when certain deeds are done, we'll meet again."

He pushed me out of the tunnel, his laughter following me as I returned to life.

Part of my work as a psychic medium comes from families desperate to contact loved ones who have passed away. Most of the time, these are not good deaths. They are people who have died suddenly—through something like accident, suicide, or murder—or who have died while distanced from their relatives by some force, like drugs or estrangement. Always, there are things left unsaid. That is where I come in. I am the communications link between the two sides. The living and the dead. And helping one side also helps the other. I have stopped being surprised at how much both sides still have to say, even after it's too late. So then they find me—because I help it be never too late.

I have spoken with the dead since I was a little girl, even before my own brush with death as a child. I know them well. I often hear people say, "No time for sleep— I'll sleep when I'm dead." I just smile to myself. If only they knew the truth: it is the living who rest. The dead don't need to. Some of them work and play, or relive their lives, or stay to comfort the grieving loved ones left behind. Some go on long journeys, traveling over hills and roads, doing everything that was restricted during life. They are free.

But some are not. This is especially true for those who die violently or much too young. They come to me the most, I think because they know I can communicate what they were robbed of the chance to say. Can you imagine walking around and having no one see or hear you, not even those you loved the most while alive? They try to get back, they try to break through. It takes a gentle hand, a kind heart, and patience to help them face what they often haven't been able to accept—their own deaths.

And so, when I meet these spirits, they give me clues about what their lives were like, signs that only their closest loved ones would recognize, so that the living will know that the spirits really are communicating through me.

I always start with a photograph. I don't go by names. It's the imprint of the face that I take with me as I go on my personal journey to the other side. I stare at the picture and sit back in my office chair. That and a bright light are all I need—none of that other fancy crap psychics on television use.

The journey usually comes with a bump. I smell flowers, or cologne, or cigar smoke—anything that was their favorite. The walls of my office often change, and the world turns into wavy lines and lights before my eyes. I look past the photo and go through the door of death. I feel weightless. The temporal world no longer holds me. I travel down that familiar tunnel. The lights turn into a steady stream, illuminating the walls as I pass crowds of people slowly walking toward me. I hear the whispers, voices reaching out to me with enduring messages.

Have you seen my son?
Tell my daddy I love him.
Tell my daughter I saw her wedding. I was right there in my favorite dress.
Has my girlfriend cried yet? I don't want to scare her by coming around.

How can the living think that the dead don't feel? The body is just a house for a short time. The soul lives forever. When they come through me, I begin to write. After I get what I need, I pull myself out as fast as I can. Sometimes their sufferings are more than I can bear. The pain of the families and the dead is now mine as well. If only I had the ability to prevent such tragedies, to bring the dead back. But, unfortunately, death is an industry that never stops.

And I can never say no. So I was at work two days into the new year, my holiday break over. I sat in my office and stared at the photograph of a middle-aged man. The attached note from his children and sister said he had passed away almost three years earlier. They hoped to make contact with him.

I had three hours before their call. I didn't need that much time to travel to the beyond and back. I stared at his face. "What happened to you?" I asked out loud. This time, there was no bump, no scent of the past. I went through the door anyway, and down that tunnel. I searched and searched, but I knew I would not find him. I kept going because I wanted to have something to tell the grieving family. But he was not there.

Gradually, the crowds of people thinned until there was no one, and the empty tunnel began to echo with dripping water. The floor started to feel thick and pulled at my feet, making my footsteps heavy and unsure. A ball came bouncing toward me—the red rubber ball of a child—and I looked toward the end of the tunnel to see a little girl in a yellow raincoat appear. The sludgy water dripped all around her, but not a drop actually touched her. She covered her eyes and cried out for her mother. She choked back her sobs and looked at me. "Will you please play with me?"

As she spoke, a light shone behind her like a storm had lifted and the heavens were smiling down. I took a step forward, but my Forever Guardian—my younger self who died on the operating table and has continued to appear to me throughout my life, protecting me always—stopped me and told me not to go. I stood with her and looked at the little girl in the raincoat, who waited there at the end of the tunnel for my decision. I hesitated, and my Forever Guardian yanked me back. I fell into the air, twisting and turning, then landed with a thump in my own office chair. I gasped for breath and held my now-pounding head. I looked down and saw that my feet were covered with mud and slime from my journey. I staggered into the bathroom and threw some water on my face, wiped my feet off, and reached for the ibuprofen.

That was not how that travel was supposed to have gone. I did not know whom I had found, but it most definitely was not the man I'd been searching for. That family's father and brother was most definitely *not* dead. Why would his children and sister ask for this? They certainly had some explaining to do. I sat back down and began to write out my questions for them.

As I wrote, I looked at the man's photo again and began to think that I might be able to answer the questions better than his family could. I stopped taking notes and put my hand over his face. "Where are you?" I called out loudly.

I did this over and over, and slowly the answer came as the story of his life started to unfold. First I saw a little boy in a white shirt and blue short pants held up by suspenders, riding a tricycle. Then an adoring mom standing next to him at his high school graduation. I could smell the gardenia in the corsage she wore pinned to her dress. I knew I was on the right track now. His first kiss to a cute little redhead . . . his dad taking a picture of him standing alongside what I assumed had to be his first car . . . so far, the picture-perfect family life.

But then it began to change. I saw him slumped over a steering wheel, a syringe and spoon on the seat next to him . . . again and again over the years as the drugs took over . . . his attendance at what must have been a daughter's wedding, a train wreck of a father bringing no joy . . . a flash of his family, sitting in a kitchen and mourning what they thought was his death . . . and then there he was, sitting on a park bench with some other homeless people. Yes, he was definitely one of them—dirty clothes, ripped sneakers and no socks to cover his swollen ankles, a cigarette butt behind his ear, wrapped in a worn blanket. He showed signs of schizophrenia, which is very common for someone living in those conditions. My heart went out to him. A lost man at rock bottom, huddled in the cold, thinking no one cared anymore.

I looked at the bench, at the city around him, and sat up straight in astonishment. It was Union Square Park, near Greenwich Village, in the city. It was no more than a thirty-minute train ride from my house. Man, did I have a wonderful belated Christmas gift for this family! Their father and brother was alive, and we could help him. I would gladly give my assistance in reuniting them.

I put down the pen with which I had furiously been taking notes and pushed the intercom button to speak to my daughter, Joanne. "Get this family on the phone now! I have good news for them!"

Her voice came back at me. "Are you kidding me? You always change the schedule." I knew I had other people waiting to see me. "It takes me days to fit people in," she said.

I knew that. I knew how I made her work as my assistant much more difficult. I was always changing things up at the last minute. And that wonderful daughter of mine is always my miracle worker, somehow finding a way to make everything still run smoothly. As she did again this time—the family called me within five minutes.

We greeted each other, and I could tell that I was on speaker phone. Normally, I hate that. I feel a reading is very personal, and I should be talking only to that person, not a whole audience.

But in this case, everyone on the other end of the phone wanted to know about their dear, "departed" father and brother. I saw them sitting around a kitchen table, passing a box of tissues before the questions started.

"Does he have a message?"

"How is he?"

"Does he know we love him?"

As I listened to the questions, I closed my eyes and left my body, until I was standing outside a back door and looking into a kitchen. Leaning against a counter was an older man, probably in his eighties but still quite sharp. He looked a little nervous. Ah, that was because he was wanting me—on the other end of the phone line—to prove him right. He was the one who had arranged this reading for his son's daughters and sister. He wanted me to say some otherworldly gibberish, some kind of hogwash, and confirm that his son was dead. His very much alive and homeless son.

Well, since I am not a fraud, I was unable to do what he had hoped that I would. I opened my eyes and was back in my office. I stopped the family's questions with one of my own.

"Who is the older gentleman standing to the back of you?"

I could feel them turning around and looking at him as if to say, "How did you know that?" Now that I had their full attention, I began to explain about their son, father, and brother. I described his whereabouts, his drug use, his likely mental illness, his desperate need of help. I could hear the tears falling on the other end of the phone. One daughter said she always had a feeling that he was still alive. They had been told he had died in an accident years ago. I asked why there was no funeral, and they said that their grandfather had taken care of the arrangements and felt it best to just have him quickly cremated.

There were heavy questions in the air around that kitchen table. The grandfather began to yell. "I don't need this. I gave you girls everything that deadbeat son of mine couldn't." I could feel his pain. In a way, he was right. He gave everything he could, and he couldn't forgive his son. Instead of the joy I'd expected, I ended the call feeling horrible for everyone involved.

The grandfather contacted me the next day to instruct me to leave things alone. In his eyes, his son had died a long time ago. I tried to talk to the daughters. They said they were happy to know that their father was not dead, but there was nothing they could do for him alive. And then they hung up. I was left confused by the whole situation. How could they have this new knowledge and not act on it?

This was such an unusual result for me. I almost never get to deliver the news that there is life instead of death. I don't often get to tell people that amends can be made now, in this world, before anyone crosses over to the other side. I rarely get to tell clients that they still have time and can do the communicating on their own.

Maybe that was why I couldn't let it rest. This poor man needed help, and I felt I'd been brought into his story for a reason. Two days after his family told me to do nothing more, I set out for Union Square Park to do more anyway. I don't like seeing people in pain. Helping the vulnerable is one of my own vulnerabilities. And unfortunately for me, there were those who knew this.

I took a pack of smokes and some coffee with me. I know the currency of the streets, and a few cigarettes can usually buy you some information. I walked through the whole area, looking everywhere. I saw crack vials, empty dope bags, tiny specks of blood on the ground. I showed the man's photograph around, though most of these people wouldn't have recognized the guy if he were sitting on their laps.

I kept searching as the winter sun went down and dark clouds moved in. I finally sat down on a bench, about to admit defeat in my search for this nowhere man, when I happened to notice the feet of the person sitting next to me, wearing the same torn sneakers I'd seen in my vision three days earlier. I peeked into the blanket he wore wrapped around himself and got a look at his face. Jackpot! I told myself to remain calm. I did not want to spook him. I slowly pulled out a cigarette and extended it toward him. An aged, soiled hand emerged from the blanket and snatched it from my fingers. I lit it for him and watched the smoke billow from his nose and mouth.

"What do you want from me?" he said. "You a cop?"

"No. I'm no cop," I said carefully.

He peered around his blanket at me with a very alert expression in his eyes. "Well, I ain't going home, and I ain't going with you. This is no place for you. Go away."

Yeah, everyone knows how well *that* works on me. I knew of a men's shelter where he could get medical care. "I want to help you. Please, let me get you a warm bed, some food, and a hot shower, and then we can talk."

He stood up and flung the half-smoked cigarette away. I stood up quickly, too, and said, "You have a family that loves you. You owe it to your daughters and yourself."

He stopped, and I thought for a split second that I'd gotten through to him with the power of remembrance and love. Then he began to chuckle, and in a different voice—one that sounded like a bucket of stones being dumped into the well of my soul—he said, "You couldn't save your poor, tormented mother and you want to save me. You will always be a slave to salvation, you pitiful idiot."

I know the devil talking when I hear it. I yanked the blanket off him and found myself staring not at the son and father I'd been searching for but some man in his thirties with long blond hair and track marks mapping his arms. That sudden movement attracted the attention of the many homeless people, and they began to move toward me. I knew I had to get out of there. I bolted and was almost away when I ran right into a tall man dressed all in black. He had coal-black eyes and hair, short except for a thin ponytail that hung over his shoulder. He grabbed both of my arms. "You could get hurt stalking people," he said. He pulled me into him, and I could feel his breath on my cheek. He rubbed his lips up my face to my ear.

"Now we are one," he whispered. "We are one. Two is one."

I wrenched myself free and ran to the subway. The thirty-minute ride back felt like eternity—I had never been so glad to see home. My husband, Will, greeted me at the door and asked me where I'd been.

"I don't know," I said, "but something is coming."

TWO

I was working too hard. That was all it was, I kept telling myself. That was why this spirit was tugging at the edges of my brain, slipping past the corner of my eye, following me, and then disappearing as soon as I turned to look. Wrong numbers would appear on my cell phone and come back as disconnected when I called them. My voice mail would fill with incoherent messages. There would be knocks on the front door and no one outside when I answered.

Food that I loved now turned my stomach. I would awaken in the middle of the night and stare at Will, wondering who he was and how I could get him to leave. My friends started to complain that I was acting differently, talking differently, dressing differently. I ate with my hands in restaurants, even fancy ones, which was a breach of etiquette my Southern upbringing would never, ever allow. I would catch myself in outfits that looked more like hooker-chic than my usual modest dress. I would glimpse myself in a mirror and wonder who had styled my hair or put on my makeup. It certainly wasn't me.

Jewelry went missing. Not my everyday stuff but expensive pieces I usually wore only once or twice a year. I would find them stashed far in the back of my armoire, under piles of clothes. When I straightened up the house, I would fluff a throw pillow and put it on the left side of a living room armchair. The second I let go of it, it would lift up and smash down on the right side. If I switched it back, the same thing would happen. Music would suddenly start blasting from the turned-off stereo. My cell phone, which I placed fully charged on my bedside table at night, would be completely drained of power every morning. I finally took it back to the store and was told that there was nothing wrong with it.

Some nights, I would jolt awake from a dead sleep, consumed with overwhelming fear. I felt like I was being watched very closely, as though something were inches from my face. Other nights, I didn't wake up at all. But in the morning, instead of pajamas, I would awake to find myself in jeans and a T-shirt that reeked of booze and stale cigarette smoke, my feet covered with mud. Where had I been walking?

I got messages on my phone from strangers telling me that they'd had fun and asking if we could get together again. They never left names, and I quickly got in the habit of deleting them so my family wouldn't find out. Many of my appointments—both personal and professional—got canceled, and when I asked about it, the people I had been scheduled to meet with said I was the one who had done it. I never had any memory of doing so.

I kept trying to work throughout these months. I am a psychic medium, and I interact regularly with people who are grieving or traumatized, so I always take great care to be respectful and kind when I communicate. But now, when I typed out e-mails to my clients, I found myself unconsciously inserting words in the middle of my sentences.

Help me.
I'm inside.
Murder.
He's coming.
Beware.
Killer.
I'm stuck in an asylum.

None of these phrases had anything to do with what I was actually writing. I would stare at a completed e-mail in total confusion. Where was this coming from?

I slowly began to feel that I was losing control of my own life. Did I still even have one? One day, as I was saying good-bye to my husband as he headed off to work, I looked out our front door. The world outside was black and gray. *Maybe I'm dead, and he's afraid to tell me.* I had known spirits who had not yet figured out that they had really died. Was I one of them? The thought turned me cold, and Will stepped back from our hug as though he felt the chill.

He knew me so well, my big bear of a husband. And

he knew other things, too. He was educated in voodoo mysticism, just as I was, and understood the other world that always called to me. He had always been able to tap into my thoughts and emotions telepathically, but now he looked unsure as he stared at me in our foyer.

I first saw Will when I was in my late teens, as he climbed aboard a streetcar in New Orleans. My eye was immediately caught by the tall, handsome black man with a voodoo protection symbol tattooed on his chest. I would see him occasionally in different places in the city, but I did not learn his name for several years.

At that point, in my early twenties, I was traveling the world, helping tend to wounded souls. The elders in New Orleans's small voodoo community began to worry about my safety and thought that having a protector would be smart. So they suggested someone accompany me on my travels, and introduced me to that streetcar passenger I had seen before. And Will Barrett and I became inseparable.

He watched over me and my daughter, Joanne, as all three of us became seasoned globetrotters.

He started asking me to marry him after we had been traveling together for about a year. I said no. He kept asking, and I kept saying no. I liked things the way they were. We were best friends, and I knew I could depend on him for my life. I didn't need a marriage certificate for that. Plus, I didn't want to put him in danger by linking him to me that way.

But that man wouldn't give up. He asked me for about the hundredth time on Saint Valentine's Day in 1997. It was a cold day in New Orleans, and I felt at that very moment an even colder blast run right through my bones. I knew it was time to make things right. So we got married in a voodoo ceremony that night in the Saint Louis Cemetery on North Rampart Street. He gave me a beautiful snake ring that symbolizes the white serpent of healing. And I gave him a ring that belonged to my father, a Blackfoot medicine man. We've been together for more than twenty-five years. He has made my work his work, and with him, I never felt scared or alone.

Until now. Will looked at me closely as he left for work and told me I was working too hard. I needed a break. Take a few days off. Maybe I was still among the living and not dead after all. As he walked down the path and away, I paused to look around at my front garden, which was slowly returning to color from the black and gray of minutes before. Even though we lived in New York now, I'd kept my New Orleans green thumb. Green twisting vines with big pink blooms grew up the front wall, and other plants surrounded the double-tiered fountain just outside the front doors. Everyone in the neighborhood seemed to enjoy it. A little bit of nature always makes things better.

And then there was my gate. I had designed it myself and collaborated with an artist and an iron worker to make it. It would have made my father, an iron worker himself, proud. A small cross sat on top of each picket, and the middle came together in a much larger cross—although you would have to walk across the street in order to be far enough away to realize that. There also were voodoo *veves*—the symbols of protection and love. I guess I'd brought more with me from New Orleans than just my green thumb.

I walked out into my garden, happy I could now see the pink of the flowers. Could I still feel them? I reached out and grabbed one tightly. Yes, thank goodness. The flower filled my hand, and I could feel every part of it. But when I let go, the bright petals started to fade and shrivel as they fell to the ground. By the time they reached the earth, they were dead. I touched one slightly with my foot, and it sounded like I had just stepped on broken glass.

"You killed it!"

I jumped and whirled around. The screech had been full of fury, but there was no one behind me. I looked out the gate. There was no one there, either.

I went back into the house, my heart racing. My hands were covered with pink from the petals and yellow from the flower's stamen. I walked into the kitchen to wash them. I soaped up, and the colors began to wash down the drain. Then came the blood. I looked my hands over, but there were no cuts anywhere. Yet the more I rinsed them, the more blood poured forth.

I grabbed a dish towel and dried my hands and arms. I had to get a second one to wipe the sink and the counter. Finally I seemed to have gotten it all. I used one more towel to scrub everything with bleach and then tossed all three—soaked with blood—into a bag. I didn't know what to do with them, so I took them down the block to a service laundry that I always use. I walked up to the counter, and the woman there eyed my small bag.

"Is this it?" she asked.

I looked around nervously. I did not want anyone to see my red-stained towels.

"I had a bit of an accident and cut myself," I said. I knew this sounded odd, considering there was not a mark or a bandage on me. I pulled out one of the balled-up towels. "Please do your best to get the blood out. I just got these towels, and they're expensive."

She took the bag from me and pulled out the other two towels. I was paying more attention to the people around me, wondering what they were thinking about me.

"Miss Jackie," the woman said. From her tone, she must have been trying to get my attention repeatedly. She held up one of the towels.

"There is no blood—nothing. Only heavy bleach. I can wash them for you."

I grabbed the towels and turned them over frantically, wanting to validate what had just happened to me. There was nothing. Only bleach.

After months of whispers and thumps and a disembodied voice, I finally started seeing the culprit. She would appear on the street and go darting through traffic. I would see my own reflection in the glass of a store window and then hers right behind me. Once I walked downstairs and found her sitting in my office chair, wearing the same lucky red sweatshirt I had just put on. Another time, she made me take a drink. I fought my own hand as it brought the alcohol up to my mouth. I've never been a drinker, and it immediately made me sick. I ran into the bathroom to throw up and found her sitting on the counter, where she babbled away incoherently as I hung over the toilet. I could make out some words—she said that she was beautiful, and the two of us had work to do. She passed me a tissue so I could wipe my mouth and laughed at me. I felt sicker than ever.

I knew she was dead. But I did not know who she was or what she wanted. Did she want help? Did she want my body, my life?

Even my most mundane actions, my boring errands, were not exempt. I couldn't even make an ordinary trip to the grocery store, for goodness' sake, walking out to find the blue sky turning to deep gray. The air was thick, and the trees began to sway in the increasing wind. I quickened my steps, hoping to make it the six blocks home before the sky opened up.

"Jackieeee . . ."

The word was whispered directly into my ear. I spun around, expecting to see someone right over my shoulder, but no one was there. The wind tugged at my clothes as I gawked at the empty sidewalk behind me. I turned and started toward home again.

"Jackieeee . . . be with me . . ."

This time there were footsteps, too, pounding the pavement behind me. I started to run. The sky cracked open and shot lightning. The way things were going, it was probably aiming directly at me. I looked up at it and lost my footing. Down I went with my bag of groceries, stupid cans spilling everywhere. And then there was stupid me, embarrassed as I got to one knee and started gathering my food. A woman stopped and bent down to help. I was starting to thank her when she took a can of beans out of my hands and began to giggle. I slid back on my knees to look up at her but couldn't see much past the matted hair obscuring her face. Just that glimpse, though, and the way she held herself sent a chill of fear down my back. What did she want with me?

"I see you're still eating this," she said, her gaze on the can of beans. She kept staring at the can and my gaze followed hers, but I focused on her hand—gray flesh and chewed fingernails embedded with dirt and blood. She saw my look and dropped the can, swinging her hand behind her back.

"Don't you look at me like that!" She started sobbing and licking her lips. "It wasn't my fault!" Her breath came in heaves, and I moved back, trying to put some space between us. I finally realized that no one else could see her. All the people rushing past me, crouched on the sidewalk, were not aware of the woman at all. I knew I had taken one step beyond that door of mine that swings both ways as often as it wants to.

"Do I know you?" I asked softly. "Why are you following me?"

She stood up and kicked over my poor grocery bag. "Take your stuff and get the fuck away from me." Then she used one hand to cover her face while the other tugged at her dirty pants, reminding me of a shameful child trying to hide. I suddenly felt sorry for her.

"Don't cry," I said. "I'm sorry if I hurt your feelings."

I stood slowly and carefully picked up my last few scattered cans, trying not to move quickly and set her off again. "Why do you follow me?" I asked.

"Because you know me. We're the same, can't you see?"

With that, she swung toward the busy avenue and bolted into traffic. "Race you home!" she yelled over her shoulder. I grabbed my groceries and raced after her, reflexively yelling for the cars to stop. I shoved past people waiting for the light to change and then stopped and reminded myself that I was the only one who could see her. The people behind me began to whisper about the crazy lady, meaning me. *It isn't me, it's her*, I wanted to yell. The light changed and I ran, away from the whispers and toward home.

I burst through my front door and saw the alarm was still set. She hadn't gotten in. Or had she? Who was this woman? I kicked the door shut and dropped my now-trashed bag of groceries onto the floor.

"I know you're in here. Come out and show yourself," I said. My bedroom door slammed shut.

Now I was actually scared. This had never happened to me before. I bolted into the kitchen and dug a knife out of the silverware drawer. Sweat from my run—and my fear—dripped down into my eyes. I wiped it away and took a breath. That small action gave me pause. What the hell was I doing? Standing in my own kitchen holding a knife like Norman Bates and shrieking at a ghost? I had to get a grip. I put down the knife and began to walk slowly down the hallway to my bedroom. As I approached, the door cracked just a bit, and my beloved cat Oreo shot out past me. She raced to the living room and started scratching at the glass French doors that led out to the front yard.

I followed her and tried to scoop her up into my arms. I had to drop down on all fours and crawl after her as she scooted around a folding screen and kept scratching and meowing at the window. I knew she was trying to show me something, and I was damn sure I didn't want to see what it was. I finally got my arms around her and started to slide backward, away from the French doors. She clawed at me, and I let her go as I stared up and outside. What I saw froze me with fear. A tall man dressed all in black stood on the other side of the door. His face was covered with a rag, which he lifted in order to press his mouth against the glass. His breath frosted the pane before he stepped back slightly and let the rag fall back into place.

"Jackie," I heard him say, as if he were in the room with me, "give me what belongs to me."

I crawled away as fast as I could, trying to keep from being pulled into a fight I had nothing to do with.

As this woman kept stalking me, I tried desperately to live a normal life. Well, normal for me. My job as a psychic medium isn't exactly something you find in the "help-wanted" section of the paper. I use my skills in many ways, not all of them related to death. I help the love struck decide whether their infatuations are truly right for them. I help guide artists and performers toward their next projects. I help families find relatives who have been lost to the streets and the ravages of drugs. I guide people on their deathbeds over to the other side. I help law enforcement with homicide and missing-person cases. And I help those robbed of loved ones by murder or suicide have that last conversation they would otherwise be denied.

But along with the good always comes the bad. Through my work, I also am acquainted with the devil. I have witnessed and participated in true exorcisms. I have come face-to-face with demons. I have always stood up to them, resisted their leader. I feel that the devil is always looking for a way in with me. Always searching for a crack, some way to slip past my defenses. Maybe my gift is what he wants. A fine soldier I would be in his army. He knows my qualifications.

I am the combination of two bloodlines rich in the supernatural. My father was a Blackfoot Indian who knew the earth and its rhythms. He was connected to everything natural, and he used those links to stay within the good and the right. He did not walk in the darkness. His view of the worlds—both this one and the next—was expansive, and he taught me to notice what most others did not. Each thing had a purpose, and if I knew that, I could open my mind to its other possibilities. He taught me how to summon our ancestors and ask them for guidance, and he brought me to my special protector, the spirit wolf assigned to me at birth who has guarded me ever since. And he taught me how to treat everyone—no matter what their station in life—with respect.

My father was a huge man, big and strong. He worked

with his hands all his life, molding steel and iron into all sorts of things, pipelines and bridges, and swinging a sledgehammer most men couldn't even lift. He came down from Canada and met my mother in New Orleans. Where else would she be, my voodoo high-priestess mother? She was of Sicilian descent, but she was Bayou through and through, an expert in the humid byways and old mysticism of the South. She spent her life ridding other people of their demons, but what she vanquished also fascinated her. In the end, the dark proved too tempting and too powerful. My mother trapped a very strong demon, but rather than damning it back to hell, she tried to set it forth to work for her. Instead, it consumed her, and even an exorcism could not defeat it. It took me years to accept that my own mother had succumbed while in an abandoned hotel on Coney Island, where even two priests and a nun could not overcome the demon inside her.

The exorcism had been going on for days when I got there, just in time to see my mother floating in the middle of a blood-spattered room. Her empty eyes showed the empty space where her soul had been, forever eaten by the devil. She had lost. In her work—her communications with the dead, her ridding others of demons—she had lost. And ever since, I have lived in fear that the same thing would happen to me.

The woman who had been haunting me finally introduced herself one night at the movies. I walked into the theater restroom, and the fluorescent lights began to dim. The row of toilets began to flush all at once, and the faucets ran to overflowing. I started breathing heavily, and saw the frost of my exhale come from my mouth like Arctic air. I went into a stall and sat down, praying that I could just go to the bathroom in peace. Then an invisible hand scratched letters into the back of the door, right in front of my face.

P-A-T-R-I-C-I-A.

I felt faint. My heart thudded in my chest, and my breath froze my lips. I had to get out of there. I pushed open the stall door and ran toward the exit as the toilets started to overflow. Water spilled everywhere. I felt like I was going to pass out. I reached the exit, and although I barely had the strength, I peeked behind me. Nothing was out of place. All I saw was a silent, clean, dry bathroom. I stood still for a moment, shaking, and then looked in the mirror. It cracked, splitting my reflection in two.

THREE

———

I had coffee in my hand and headphones in my ears as I descended into the subway. My music blocked out the chitchat around me as I waited for the R train. I was on my way to one of my favorite little cafés down on the Lower East Side to meet an artist friend of mine for a late breakfast so we could talk about his upcoming project.

Many artists run their ideas by me so I can give them the vibe I get about their concepts, enlightening them about what will come. I always meet these clients in person. They need to look into my eyes and sit with me to create the spark of inspiration. We go into a meditative state together. This allows them to let go of any physical pain. Any emotional pain, of course, goes into their creation. What is art without tears of the heart? To the public, it might just seem like a beautiful piece, but to the artists, it is nothing less than a slice of their soul.

This wonderful friend of mine had just yesterday come

to my office, which is one of the best places to do a ritual circle. My black mirror and altar are surrounded by antiques and illuminated by a red crystal chandelier. The light bathes the purple walls, red-leather couch, and leopard-print rug. The two of us sat on the couch and held hands to exchange creative energy. We stared into each other's eyes, and his hands became electric. It was as if every one of his unanswered questions fell into place at that very moment. This is a must with artists—visualizing every step as the process begins.

The energy was so intense that the two of us started dancing. We blasted music and recordings I have of war drums, and we painted our faces with Native American markings. We danced around the office as he opened up his spirit, which was exactly my intent. I know very well that the spirit moves the body and feeds the mind. Now my toes tapped to the music on my iPod as I waited for my train and remembered the day before. We had really rocked it out, and I'd felt great about helping him continue his increasingly successful career. We'd worked together for more than sixteen years and now just needed to finalize plans for his show over coffee. I love this part of my work. Who wouldn't? It's so positive, so full of anticipation and promise.

The roar of the approaching train interrupted my thoughts. It looked empty, and I initially thought it would blow right through the station like all out-of-service trains do. But it began to slow, and I automatically moved toward it. No one joined me. Everyone else on the platform continued with their conversations and didn't even glance toward the train. That *never* happens here in New

York. There's always a hurried jostling, maybe even a little shoving, as people rush for the seats.

The train screeched to a stop, and the doors banged open. My logical mind told me not to get on that train, but my feet worked by themselves, almost tripping me as they carried me through the doors. I really had no choice. I hesitantly walked onto the train, and the doors slammed shut behind me. Everyone else stayed on the platform. The train lurched forward, and I looked around. There were four homeless people with me in the car. All of them were sleeping, curled around plastic garbage bags that I guessed held all of their worldly possessions. One guy clutched a small transistor radio, held together with rubber bands. I sat across from him and looked down at my iPod, thinking how fortunate some of us are.

I continued to sit there, almost transfixed. I paid no attention to the stops, or to whether the train even stopped at all. It rocked from side to side as it went even faster. An empty bottle of whiskey rolled out from under a seat and bumped its way down the speeding train until it hit my shoe. I slowly lifted my foot to let it pass, but it stayed where it was. *Why doesn't it roll down the aisle?* I wondered. The train was moving so fast, *I* would roll down the aisle if I stood up.

I kicked the bottle underneath my seat and tried to shake off my stupor. I shut off my iPod, hoping to hear the conductor announce an upcoming stop. But there were none. The train was going through a dark tunnel, and all I could see were flashing red and blue lights that made me dizzy. I got up to get a better look at the tunnel graffiti and realized that the train was on the middle track, the express track, and was not going to stop.

A sound came from behind me, and I remembered the homeless people with whom I shared the car. I turned and saw them still asleep, but an old newspaper blew through the air toward me. As I bent down to look at it, it stopped moving, as though it was trying to show me something.

WOMAN FOUND DEAD, PATRICIA FONTI,
AUGUST 10, 1992, AT THE AGE OF 39

I glanced around the car, thinking that someone was playing a joke on me. I picked up the newspaper and walked over to the sleeping man with the transistor radio.

"Is this a joke? Did you do this?" I demanded, waking him up. "Look at it!"

I was so upset I couldn't help myself. I moved to the center of the train car. "Who did this to me?" I yelled, waking everyone up.

The radio man looked at me like I was crazy, which set me off even more. He took a pair of broken reading glasses out of his pocket, put them on, and looked at the paper I shoved at him.

"What is this?" I demanded again. "Look at the year."

"1992," he answered.

Fear settled in me. "What year is this?"

A chorus answered me. All four of the homeless people said in unison, "It's August 1992."

What? The year 1992 was more than twenty years ago. I threw the newspaper down and sank into a seat, cradling my head in my hands and rocking back and forth. "Wake up. You just have to wake up. This isn't real," I chanted to myself. I stayed huddled in that position until I felt the train begin to slow. I raced back to my window and peered out again. This time, I saw a long arrow painted on the tunnel wall. My eyes followed its direction, and outside in the tunnel I saw a small group of people squatting together and sobbing. The train slowed almost to a stop, as if it wanted me to see every detail of their torment. They were all in robes. One woman's back was exposed, and I could count every rib through her gaunt flesh.

And then I saw him, a dark figure standing over the group. I could not make out his face even though I pressed my cheek against the glass of the train window, straining to get a look at him. But I knew who he was. I had seen him darting in and out of dark places for years. He had appeared in my dreams, pulling me toward a dark psychic cesspool. The tall man in black. The devil. And now he was so close. He pointed down the tunnel as the train moved forward again, this time with the rhythmic clack of a roller coaster straining toward its highest point. He continued to point, and I continued to be carried away. Clack, clack, clack.

Suddenly the train stopped, and I honestly thought it was preparing for a roller-coaster drop into hell. I looked around frantically and saw through the windows that an opening had appeared in the tunnel, and out of it rolled an old wooden wheelchair. Leather-strap restraints hung off the arms and swung wildly as it turned toward me. Its wheels squeaked as it rolled closer.

It looked like a torture device, something used to imprison poor, crazy people. It terrified me. I stumbled back from the window and fell. The radio man gathered his meager belongings and knelt next to me.

"Well, Jackie, this is my stop. This is where I belong," he said. "You can't run. There's nowhere to hide. You are going to have to face this one." He stood. "It's been real nice seeing you, Jackie."

He turned and walked right through the door. Now I could see the bullet hole in the back of his head. The others followed him. I sat on the floor and watched soul after soul pass through the train door and walk into the tunnel. The radio man slowly turned and waved at me. "Don't stray from the path or you won't be able to come back. Stay on that line."

I dropped my head onto my knees and sobbed. Who could I turn to? Why couldn't I be like other people? Why was I forced to have this existence? Why?

The train stopped hard, jolting my body. I looked up to find myself in a normal, packed subway car, full of New Yorkers going about their business. Everyone in their own worlds. If they only knew about mine.

I had no conception of how much time had passed. I did not remember I had an appointment. I did not know where I was going once I got off the R train. My feet just carried me, block after block.

Standing at an intersection, I saw a woman waving wildly at me from across the street, yelling at me to cross even though traffic flew by. She waved and yelled, but no one else saw her. This was the woman who had been watching me for so long now. Patricia. The one who had been waiting.

The light changed, and I ran across the street to her, though she also ran, toward a huge stone building. I stopped and stared. The old Bellevue insane asylum, now a homeless shelter. Dead, twisted vines crawled up the stone and broken brick, as though massive tree roots stretched upward to cover the entire building. I saw Patricia disappear inside, and I could not follow. I knew I should, I knew I needed to see where she was leading me, but I couldn't do it. I stood on the sidewalk, at war with myself, feeling like one of the schizophrenics who used to call this horrific building home.

I stared up at the fortress and saw the torn curtains in one window swing open and that same old wooden wheelchair roll into view. And I saw myself strapped into it. The tall man in black I had seen in the tunnel was pushing me.

"We're waiting for you, Jackie," he bellowed. His face was covered with a mask that completely covered his head in black. A white circle went around the edges of where his face must be, and a white cross went through the middle of that. The sign of the zodiac. On the street below, I could hear him start to laugh. "Accept your inheritance and come forward. Don't you want to play? It's not over until I say it is."

I lay in bed, safe in my own house, wondering what awaited me today. I had not recovered from yesterday's

train ride to hell, and I knew it wouldn't be my last contact with that horrible tall man in black. Traveling through
different dimensions was as easy for me as walking to the
drugstore, but I'd always been able to control that path-
way before. I had built it, after all, and I thought it was
mine to travel according to my own will. Now I was being
shown otherwise.

I knew what was happening to me. I was no stranger
to the signs of possession. Lost souls had always lived
alongside me. But now this one was within me. I was
being pursued and taken over. I was getting beaten up
from within. Two souls cannot share one body for more
than a short period of time. If they do, the person whose
body it is can be irreparably harmed. It can cause severe
psychiatric problems like split personality or psychosis.

Just how long can the human body keep this up? I asked
myself. A voice I did not recognize answered me.

"For as long as we want."

I laughed. There was little else I could do. There were
now squatters sharing my soul.

I did not know how much time passed, but the voices
quieted, and then my two cats were with me, affection-
ately rubbing my face. I closed my eyes and felt the vibra-
tion of their purring. Such a normal experience. A
wonderful, beautifully normal experience. I filled with
joy as I tossed back the covers and went into the bathroom
to brush my teeth. I told myself in the mirror how wonderful it was to be back in my own body with my own
thoughts.

I followed my girls to the kitchen, where they demanded

breakfast. I poured bowls of their favorite food and fresh water and then put on the coffee for myself. I hummed as I got my favorite stained and chipped cup out of the cabinet. I loved this old cup. Older is always better. I have learned the hard way that you can't wash history away. Better to accept it—stains, chips, and all.

I still had trouble believing that this perfect normalness was real. I couldn't resist peeking over my shoulder as I poured my first cup. I blew the steam off the top and leaned against the counter, smiling as my two girls devoured their food. Then a cold breeze slipped by me like a thief trying to sneak in unnoticed. The air in front of me bent into a crooked wave. The cats began to hiss and fight, which they never did. Then they ran for cover as the sound of knocking came from the front door.

The first one was gentle, as if a child were on the other side. I moved cautiously toward the door, which was solid oak in a reinforced frame. The next knock was a ringing clap, the sound of a sledgehammer hitting metal. I thought the door would shatter as I crept closer and looked through the peephole.

An older lady stood smiling at me. "Good morning, dear," she said in a sweet voice.

"Please go away," I said, shaking and sweating on the other side of the door.

"I'm spreading the word of God, you know. He knows you're in need."

I looked through the peephole again and she met me there, her eye looking right back at mine. "Jesus loves you, oh yes, he does."

Tears rolled down my face. How I needed to hear those words. I managed to ask her name.

"Why, my name is Sally," she said. "I just want to give you this pamphlet. It may just save you. He sent me right to your door." She shook the paper at me, knowing I was still watching behind the door. "My child, I have more to fear than you—a little ole gal like myself spreading the Good Word."

I straightened my clothing and tried to get the courage to open the door. Sally continued to talk in that beautiful voice. "Jesus loves you, yes, he does, 'cause the Bible says he does . . ."

I froze. The phrase was wrong. Such a simple one to know, and it was off. Demons never got it right. I flung open the door and stepped outside—wanting to confront her, wanting someone solid I could grab and demand an answer from for everything that was going on. There was no one there. Her pamphlet was stuck on the door. I ripped it off and tore through the empty pages until I got to the last one. In red crayon, scrawled like a child had written it, were the words, "Stay dead. Stay dead."

I knew then I couldn't stop it. I couldn't just go back inside and be safe. So I decided to walk right into it, whatever it was.

I turned and walked out my front gate and into a great space, enclosed in darkness. Then the lights came on, big fluorescent ones, one at a time. It was another tunnel, lined with mirrors. The light bounced everywhere, and I moved farther in, pushing on the mirrored walls with the hope of finding a door that would lead me back to my own world. Then I heard the keys.

Jingling keys and a rolling cart. One wall of mirrors became transparent, and through it I could see a nurse with grayish-brown hair and chipped teeth as brown as wood, pushing that cart down a pitiful hallway of dingy green paint and water stains. I noticed that the cart was full of medications, and the hallway was full of locked doors. I followed her along on my side of the mirrors as she screamed at the people who must be behind those doors. She stopped and unlocked door number 7, then turned and looked in my direction.

I was still on my side of the mirror, frozen in place. I squeezed my eyes shut and hoped the nurse couldn't see me. I peeked, which always gets me into trouble. I should know better by now, but honestly, every time I really have no choice. When I looked, I saw that the woman stood staring at me; then she smirked and followed my gaze down to her name tag.

"Ha. Yeah, that's my name. Nurse Sally to you." Her smirk stayed in place. "Oh dear, and you thought Jesus loved you."

She started to laugh, but she suddenly had a man's voice. She turned and went into room 7, her man's voice trailing after her. "Keep going, Jackie. You came for a reason."

That was it. I panicked, running from mirror to mirror but seeing only tragedy and pain. I heard something coming toward me, again from the other side. It was the old wooden wheelchair, coming to collect what was left of me.

But I wasn't the one strapped to it this time. Another woman sat there in a ripped and filthy hospital gown. She pushed back her matted hair and shamefully pulled her torn gown together to cover her exposed breast. We stared at each other, and she slowly put her hand out as though she could touch me. I did the same. I saw a hospital ID band around her wrist. To my surprise, there was an identical one around my wrist as well.

As our hands touched, I felt her sorrow crash through the mirror and into me. Shards of pain pierced my chest like razor-sharp teeth, plunging deep into my flesh. I closed my eyes and tried to take her agony. Her childlike whimpers became shrieking screams. They suddenly stopped, and I peeked—again. The wheelchair lay on its side, wheels spinning and covered in blood. Instead of the woman in the hospital gown's hand, through the mirror I touched the hand of the tall man in black. He was able to grasp me fully, tightly.

"You see me, Jackie, and feel me. Can you feel my power? I am god, I am the fire in hell . . . I'm the reason little boys and girls look under their beds . . . I am seeping into you, every pore of your flesh will reek of me, for I am the Gemini. I am the Two . . ."

I wrenched my hand away and ran. The mirrors started to dissolve, exposing that other side. I was running for my life. I could not let myself get stuck in hell. I ran. He yelled my name. I slipped and fell in a puddle and scrambled up. I could see home.

I ran through my front gate and found my front door wide open. I ran into my bathroom and locked the door behind me before I looked down at myself. I was covered in blood. I ripped off my pajamas, panting in fear. I was under attack, and I couldn't breathe. I grabbed a washcloth and began frantically scrubbing my arms and legs with soap and hot water.

After a while, I looked around my bathroom, puzzled and confused. My skin was raw from scrubbing with the washcloth, but there was no blood anywhere. The door was still locked, but now I could hear my cats right outside, meowing hungrily. I threw open the door and stomped into the kitchen. The coffee pot was off, and their food bowls were empty. How was this possible? I had done all of this already. I was on the verge of losing it.

"What do you want? What is it?" I yelled, waving my arms in the air. The room began to spin out of control. Or maybe it was just me. This tall man in black said he was the Gemini, that the astrological sign lived and breathed somehow. I knew that now. And he was after me. If I was the one who always helps others, who would save me? The room spun faster. I yelled for God, but that man answered.

"Now, open the door and let's play fair."

I wouldn't. I couldn't open my front door again.

"Jackie, I will blow this door in. Here I come. You can't run. You're in me. Open the fucking door!"

I screamed and sat up in bed. Wracked with pain, I leaned over the side and began to vomit. The whole thing had been a vision. My husband rushed in.

"What's wrong?" Will looked worriedly at the soiled floor and me huddled in pain. I asked him what time it was. "It's 7:30 a.m.," he answered. "I was going to let you sleep. It seems like you've been out working all night. Where were you?"

"I don't know. I don't know."

He asked if the doorbell had awoken me. I stared at him. Who was there?

"Just some old lady spreading the Good Word, I guess. You know, all the Lord stuff."

I exploded. "You didn't let her in, did you?"

"No, I didn't," he said, trying to calm me. "Come on. I'll get you some coffee."

More coffee. My God. I could no longer distinguish between what was real and what was not. My waking hours and my dreams were intertwining. And there was nothing I could do to stop it.

God help me.

FOUR

———————————

Just like any other kind of business, my psychic profession includes paperwork, filing, scheduling, and lots of other logistical duties. These things are, shall we say, not my areas of expertise. So I have an assistant who performs wondrous feats—like finding room on my calendar for all the clients who want to see me, booking the right travel arrangements, and scheduling my television and radio appearances. She is the first person anyone talks to when they try to reach me. She is my right hand, and I would never get any work done without her.

But the absolutely best thing about her? She's my daughter, Joanne. I am so lucky to get to work with her every day. And as I sat and thought about my recent visions, I knew she was just the one to help me with my latest project. We needed to figure out who Patricia Fonti was. Joanne tracks and monitors all of the paperwork for my cold cases, homicides no one has been able to solve, and she knows how important they are—she prioritizes homicide and missing-person cases when she does my scheduling. For Patricia's case, all I knew, from that headline in the newspaper that had drifted through the subway in my vision, was that she had been found dead at age thirty-nine on August 10, 1992. That seemed enough to start with, so Joanne and I sat down at the computer and started searching the Internet.

Patricia Fonti's name didn't show up in any of the usual places. No obituary. No name included in a list of local award honorees, or club members, or any of the places you can usually find some mention of a person. We couldn't even find any stories from 1992 about her death. Talk about a cold case! But then her name finally popped up—on a list of victims attributed to the New York Zodiac Killer.

Well, shit, I thought.

That discovery led Joanne and me in a whole different direction. And we slowly began to piece together the story of the hunt for one of New York's most infamous serial killers.

Not much scares New Yorkers. Certainly not back in the 1980s and 1990s, when the city saw more than two thousand murders a year, along with rampant assaults and drug dealing. It took a lot back then for a criminal to rise above the ordinary horribleness of the crime wave. But one person managed to do it, with a combination of shootings, symbols, and carefully stoked terror.

The killer started with a letter, sent to police at the end of 1989, insinuating that deaths would come the next year and would be linked to the zodiac signs. Four months later, early on a Thursday in March 1990, a forty-nine-year-old man named Mario Orozco, who had a limp and used a cane, was shot in the back while walking along a Brooklyn street. He did not die, but neither had he seen the shooter, so he couldn't give police a description.

Exactly three weeks later, again in the early hours of a Thursday, another man was shot in the back, only six blocks away from the first one. Jermaine Montenesdro was thirty-three years old. He also survived, but like Mario Orozco, he was unable to describe his attacker. The next shooting came two months later, just after midnight on a Thursday morning, this time in Queens. A seventy-eight-year-old man named Joseph Proce, who—like Mario Orozco—was using a cane to walk down the street, was approached by a man who asked him for a glass of water. Joseph started to walk away and was shot in the back. The man fled but left a letter decorated with astrological symbols nearby. Before dying of his injuries, Joseph gave police a description of his attacker as a disheveled black man in his early thirties, roughly six feet tall and about 180 pounds.

The next week, the killer sent letters to the *New York Post* and TV's *60 Minutes* naming all three victims and providing details of the shootings that only he would know. Detectives concluded that the handwriting on those letters matched the letter left by Joseph's attacker, and officially linked all three crimes.

Knowing that his letters to the media now had the cops looking for someone in the Brooklyn-Queens border area, for his next shooting, the killer traveled farther afield. He couldn't change the rest of his pattern, though. He stuck with his preference for attacking the weak and helpless, this time shooting Larry Parham, a thirty-year-old homeless man asleep on a bench in Central Park, early on a Thursday morning exactly three weeks after his previous attack, and again leaving a letter with astrological drawings nearby. This letter had a fingerprint on it, which police carefully recorded.

Larry Parham survived the shot to the chest and was able to tell the police that someone had asked for his birth date several hours before he was shot. Larry's description of the man matched the one Joseph had given three weeks earlier. For the next six years, this would be the only physical description that existed of the man police were now calling the Zodiac Killer.

So far, the killer had shot a Scorpio, a Gemini, a Taurus, and a Cancer. And he had electrified the city. People walked around in a panic. Police warned everyone to immediately report any strangers asking for their birth dates. They could not figure out how the shooter knew the signs of the first three victims. They tried in vain to link the gunman's four targets, but no connection among them was ever found. It appeared that the Zodiac struck at random, or at least did not personally know his victims beforehand, and seemed to possess knowledge he should have no way of knowing—the most terrifying combination a serial killer could have.

The killer embraced the Zodiac name and all the terror that came with it. Just after the Central Park shooting, he sent another letter to the *Post*, claiming that he was the same Zodiac who'd killed at least six people in the San Francisco area in the late 1960s. Investigators and psychologists doubted this claim from the start—the West Coast Zodiac seemed to have been a weapons expert who enjoyed torturing his victims, while the New York Zodiac kept his distance while killing, and signs pointed to his using homemade guns, since the bullets found at the crime scenes did not have characteristics typical of ones fired by properly manufactured guns. And a homemade gun would likely fire only one round, which would explain why the killer hadn't finished off his wounded victims right then and there. But the association did nothing but increase his mystique and the public's hysteria.

Psychologists guessed that the Zodiac was a poorly educated loner who probably lived alone near the Brooklyn-Queens neighborhoods where the first three shootings took place, and that he desperately wanted attention. So the police were pretty worried when the Thursday three weeks after Larry Parham's shooting rolled around, worried enough to gather a task force of fifty detectives, the largest group assembled since the Son of Sam manhunt in the mid-1970s.

That Wednesday night and Thursday morning, the task force spread throughout the city, searching for the Zodiac. They understandably concentrated in the sections of Woodhaven, Queens, and East New York, Brooklyn, where the first three attacks had occurred. And

they weren't the only ones out patrolling. Groups of cit-
izen vigilantes roamed the streets in that area, looking
for suspects. And, proving that all kinds live in New York,
still other residents actually held tailgating parties and
outdoor get-togethers to boast of being unafraid.

The police questioned more than thirty-six men
throughout that night, but none turned out to be the
Zodiac. The most famous person in New York stayed
away, still safely unknown.

No attacks came that Thursday, or the next month, or
even the next year. In fact, the Zodiac Killer waited two
years before killing again. For the first time, he used a
knife; and for the first time, he attacked on a day other
than a Thursday. Patricia Fonti was a thirty-nine-year-old
mentally ill homeless woman who frequented Highland
Park in Queens. She was stabbed more than one hundred
times just after midnight on Monday, August 10, 1992.
The amount of time that had passed, and the changes
to the killer's modus operandi, meant that her death
wasn't immediately connected to the Zodiac Killer. In
fact, like Joanne and I had found, it wasn't even reported
by most newspapers. Patricia was a Leo.

Almost a year after that, on June 4, 1993, a man named
James Weber was shot and injured near Highland
Park. It was a Friday, and he was a forty-year-old Libra.

Seven weeks later, the Zodiac Killer came back to near
Vermont and Cypress Avenues where James had been

attacked and fatally shot forty-year-old John Diacone, a Virgo.

Only five more signs to go.

The killer stayed in Highland Park for his next attack. Diane Ballard was on a park bench near Jamaica Avenue when he shot and wounded her in October 1993. She was left partially paralyzed. And she was a Taurus, the only known duplicate sign among the Zodiac's victims.

The police didn't dwell on her astrological sign, however, because they had no idea these four latest attacks were connected to one another at all. And they definitely had no clue that they had been committed by the same Zodiac Killer they'd hunted so frantically in 1990. This time, he left no letters behind, nothing to draw attention to himself.

That is, until he decided to send another letter to the *New York Post*, in August 1994.

"Hi, I'm back," it read. In it, he claimed credit for the four attacks in 1992 and 1993, as well as another one, in June 1994, that detectives could find no evidence of having actually happened. Detectives could not confirm to their satisfaction that the writer of the letter was in fact the same person who had started the reign of fear in 1990, but they knew the author at least had knowledge of the crimes that an ordinary person would not have. They were quite eager to track him down, and they hoped that a partial fingerprint left on that *New York Post* letter would help. But, having made his spectacular splash in the largest media market in the country, the Zodiac again fell silent, patiently waiting until it was time to strike again.

The police still had no idea who the Zodiac Killer was. No one did—until 1996. Then the case broke wide open. And my research got more and more interesting.

On June 18, 1996, Heriberto "Eddie" Seda was mad at his half sister. He did not like the people she was hanging out with. So he shot her. Hit in the lower back, she ran out of the family's small apartment in a drug-dealer-infested building in East New York, and someone called the police. Eddie Seda fired at the first responders from his window, which sent officers swarming all over the neighborhood, sealing off several city blocks. Residents took cover as the gunfight continued. The scale of it was unusual, but in one of the worst sections of the city at that time, gunfire was not. As one neighbor told *The New York Times*, "People know what to do around here when they hear shots."

The police negotiators eventually convinced Eddie to surrender and give up his weapons. He ended up handing over thirteen homemade zip guns, putting them into a bucket officers lowered down to his window from the roof. They were treating him as one dangerous son of a bitch, and with good reason. Once Eddie was under arrest, police found two finished pipe bombs inside his apartment, along with enough materials to make at least nine more.

Initially, the police were just relieved to have the twenty-eight-year-old in custody. But soon, they were delighted. Because Eddie couldn't help himself. At the end of a written statement about that day's standoff, he signed his name and put a strange little symbol. One of the detectives interviewing Eddie showed it to a colleague, who took one look and knew that the man who had written it was the Zodiac Killer.

The colleague had worked on the huge task force in 1990 and immediately called another detective who he knew had copies of the Zodiac letters. They compared the handwriting. Same *s*'s, same crossed *t*'s. Same guy. They went back to Eddie, who was still cooling his heels in a police station interview room. He denied it. He debated guilt and absolution with the cops for a while. Then the detectives showed him photos of his victims. Then Eddie read the Bible for a bit. And then, finally, he dictated a confession. He told them he'd had to kill his victims because they were evil.

And so Heriberto Seda was arrested in connection with eight attacks over four years. He was a recluse, a religiously devout man who railed against the drug dealers that infested his neighborhood. Growing up, his mother supported him and his half sister with welfare and small odd jobs, but she didn't maintain much control over his behavior. He still lived with both of them in that small apartment on Pitkin Avenue, where he'd stocked his tiny bedroom with the pipe bombs, along with things like a bow and arrow, plastic models of military equipment, gun magazines, and ammunition he ordered through the mail. Neighbors said he seemed to sleep all day and went out only at night. He wore black and pulled his hair back in a thin ponytail. As far as neighbors could tell, he'd never held a job and had never had any contact with his father.

His fingerprints matched the 1994 letter to the *New York Post*, as well as the print on the letter left at the scene of Larry Parham's shooting, in Central Park. Armed with that evidence and Eddie's confession, prosecutors prepared for trial.

As Joanne and I continued digging through the Internet for information on Eddie, we came across some appalling information. Eddie had been arrested before, and he could have been stopped sooner. The fingerprints left on the 1990 Parham letter and the 1994 newspaper letter had been recorded in the state law-enforcement database, ready to be compared with those of anybody arrested anywhere in New York. Unless the person was released too quickly after his arrest. Like Eddie had been.

In March 1994, five months after he'd shot and paralyzed Diane Ballard, Eddie had been arrested for carrying a gun. The cops sent it to the crime lab to see if it worked—standard procedure—and they took Eddie's prints. Back then, such things weren't transmitted immediately by computer. They'd faxed a copy of his prints to the state database, but faxed prints weren't clear enough to compare with partial fingerprints or palm prints on file. So an original set had to be sent, which usually happened within eight days of the arrest. But not with Eddie.

It turned out that his handmade gun didn't work, and the cops couldn't charge him with weapons possession. So Eddie was released, and because no charges had been filed, his original prints were destroyed before they could be sent to the state, where they could very well have triggered a match with the Parham letter. The Zodiac Killer walked out of jail with no one but him having any idea how close he'd come to being unmasked.

Eddie's first trial started in 1998, two years after his arrest. It took six weeks and involved the crimes he had committed in Queens—the murders of Joseph Proce, Patricia Fonti, and John Diacone, and the attempted murder of James Weber. Eddie sat in court and clutched a Bible most of the time. The prosecution introduced 150 pieces of evidence and called more than forty witnesses. The defense called none, instead trying to persuade jurors that their client's confession to police—which was dictated, not personally handwritten—had been coerced. They did not pursue an insanity defense, partially because they could not find any psychological expert who would testify that Eddie was insane.

The jury deliberated less than five hours before finding Eddie guilty of all three murders and the attempted murder. He was sentenced to serve at least eighty-three years and four months before becoming eligible for parole. Eddie had no reaction as the verdict was read.

One year later, he was also convicted by a Brooklyn jury of trying to kill Mario Orozco, Jermaine Montenesdro, Diane Ballard, and his own half sister, as well as for trying to shoot four police officers on the day that he was captured. For those eight convictions, Eddie was sentenced to an additional 152 years and six months in prison.

During Eddie's sentencing on the murder convictions, the prosecutor told the judge that Eddie deserved to spend the rest of his life in prison because he had purposefully created a frenzy with his letters, and because he'd intentionally targeted "lost, vulnerable souls."

Eddie became a resident of the New York State penal system in 1998. I did some quick math. That meant he wouldn't be eligible for parole until 2232, when he would be 265 years old. *Good,* I thought. *He'll never be a threat again.*

Or so I thought.

FIVE

I thought I had solved the mystery of who Patricia Fonti was, so I gratefully went back to my regular work. I still didn't know exactly what this Patricia lady wanted from me, but she quieted down a little, and I was able to get back to business. And what a business it is.

The problems that people come to see me about are as varied as the people themselves. Grieving parents and children, cops, lawyers, psychologists, petty criminals, streetwalkers, and murderers, just to name a few. And I've heard it all—personality disorders, eating disorders, sexual confusion, panic and anxiety, depression, threats of suicide, possession, reincarnation, hauntings, exorcisms.

I do my best to provide solace and relief, and sometimes I help them find their own solutions. Once clients come to see me, they become part of what I call our Universal Circle. Joanne and I keep track of their progress—the two of us meet afterward to discuss their needs and the resolution we are aiming for; then we check in with them to see how they're doing.

Some clients take more work than others. But they oftentimes turn out to be a lot of fun, too. I had one client, a successful businessman in his thirties, who could spin copper into gold but couldn't find love if it fell in his lap. He was so shy around women that the fear of speaking to one triggered bouts of irritable bowel syndrome. The thought of having a conversation with a woman he was romantically interested in would send him running for the nearest toilet, God love him. But he knew that his life was incomplete without a partner. So he came to me.

He walked into my office looking all fancy in his three-piece suit. I made him take off his shoes before we started. It teaches two things—first, never wear socks with holes, and second, that we are on even ground, with neither one of us better than the other.

His whole demeanor screamed wealth and superiority, so the first thing I did was inject a dose of reality. "Rule one, hot stuff," I said. "Ladies can make their own money, roll it out, and feed a family, too." We talked about him needing to loosen up, lose the suit and tie, and stop worrying about what others think of him.

Eventually, he admitted that he had his eye on a cute dark-haired lady in his office. I worked with him endlessly to get up the courage to ask her for a date. He thought of every scenario that could go wrong. "Right there, you are squashing your own dream," I told him. I definitely had my work cut out for me. It took two weeks of rehearsing conversations and working on his walk (to project a calm confidence), but he finally had the nerve and the skills to ask her out. She said yes. Then he went back to worrying again.

So I did my thing and made him a voodoo doll. I make my dolls from an old Louisiana-style recipe in which I stuff them with Spanish moss, herbs, roots, and some cotton to hold hand-blended oils in just the right places. I put in a piece of the owner-to-be's hair and attach a picture of the desired person to the outside. Then the doll sits on my altar for several days until the awakening happens. The doll, to a certain extent, comes to life. It becomes a part of the owner, a companion and helper. It becomes the owner's wants and needs, his best friend.

My businessman friend came for his a few days before his date. He took the tiny treasure in his hands, and as he sat down on the couch, he told me that a wave went through him and he felt light-headed. I just smiled. And then I went through the rules—he needed to visualize what he wanted in the relationship. And he could *never* use the doll for wrongdoing.

He agreed, of course, and I stepped back to have a look at him. He had the vibe. He was confident. I had a very positive vision of him in a particular Manhattan restaurant for dinner. But good grief, those clothes! We had to get him some new ones. And I knew just the guy to help us.

Gino had been my client for years. And he also happened to sell the hottest threads around out of his parents' basement in an outer borough of the city. He's a good ole Italian boy who looks like an extra in a 1970s Mob movie, living at home with his mama, and still looking for the right woman. I love going to visit—she feeds me like it was my last supper.

My client couldn't understand why we had to go all the way out there just to get a suit. He didn't want to meet anybody's family. Too nervous. I just shoved him in the car. He would be dressed to the nines in the finest sharkskin suit—that was one reason I was taking him. The other reason was because I thought it would be good for Mr. Big City Businessman to see how the other half lived.

We stopped at a bakery first, to load up on Italian cookies and bread. Being half Sicilian, I know what to do. You take food as a sign of respect. And boy, did I respect Gino's parents. The second we pulled into the driveway, they threw open the front door and greeted us with open arms. We had a huge, genuine Italian meal. His mama asked me as she served if I had a nice girl for her son. I just smiled.

After dinner, Gino and I took my client to the basement. We felt our way down the stairs and then Gino hit the lights. He has the whole place tricked out. A long oak bar with leather sides lines one wall. The middle of the room is a tiled dance floor with a big disco ball hanging over it. And on the other wall is the clothes shop, with a blue velvet curtain and full-length mirrors.

Gino put some music on, and I took a seat at the bar, coaxing my client to loosen up. Have some fun! Try stuff on! After a few hours of every color shirt and slacks, we decided on smoked silver sharkskin pants that fit like a glove and a sky-blue shirt, open at the neck. Which meant my client needed a lot less chest hair. So Gino and I broke out the wax strips . . . in hindsight, maybe not the best idea. My poor client howled in pain, and we didn't have enough to do it properly. But we ended with enough done to make the look work.

We put him in front of the mirror, and his eyes glowed. Then Gino put more music on. "Let's see what you got!" he said. We sat back and watched him dance around the floor. "Work it!" I yelled. But, oh dear. The boy had no moves at all. We decided it would be best if he kept the date to dinner and no dancing.

I told my client that no matter what he did, he had to keep his doll in his possession at all times. As he was putting it into his pocket, Gino saw it and started looking like a starved kid in a candy store.

"Oooh, you got a doll!" he said. "Let me see. Can I hold it?"

I yelled at him. No way—only the owner holds it! Gino got his pout on, turned the music off, and stomped out. My client headed to the car in silence, but I could hear what he was thinking, loud and clear—*What the hell did I get myself into?* He quickly got into the car, leaving me outside with a sulking Gino. I made peace and thanked him for making my client shine. Then I thought, *Why doesn't he help me finish it?* Come to dinner with me tomorrow, I said to Gino. I had to go to monitor my client's date. If Gino came, then he could see the results of our hard work, too.

Which was how we ended up at a table near my client and his pretty office colleague, watching them like hawks while trying to appear like we weren't looking at them at all. But I started getting frustrated. He wasn't doing what I had told him to. He wasn't even reaching for her hand. We had gone over and over this! I had to do something.

I was plotting my move when the waitress came over. "What can I get you?" she asked. "Your number," said Gino. She rolled her eyes and walked away quickly after taking our order. I kicked Gino under the table. "That's why you're alone," I hissed through my teeth. "You act like a Neanderthal!"

My client got up to use the restroom, and I immediately followed him. This was my chance to shake some sense into him. I trailed him right into the men's room and waited for him to come out of the stall.

I told him to get it together and then straightened his shirt. But the doll wouldn't fit back into his pocket because his irritable bowel syndrome had made him bloated and his pants were too tight. I told him to just stick it down his pants and go back to the table. His date was waiting for him.

I left first and sat down with Gino. So I had a great view when my client came out of the restroom with his zipper down and the voodoo doll halfway out of his pants. Heck, the whole restaurant had a great view. People's jaws dropped. Our waitress tried not to laugh.

But his date didn't see anything funny about it. My client tried to explain why he had a doll with her picture on it protruding from his crotch, but really, what can you say at that point? As the maître d' escorted him out, I shook my head in confusion. My vision of him in this restaurant had been so clear. I didn't understand it.

But then the waitress walked out with him, consoling him. She obviously thought he was adorable. That gave me something to think about. And later I found out that in all the doll-in-the-pants chaos, Gino had taken the opportunity to slip the pretty office colleague his phone number. Some may call him a weasel, but I call him slick. The last I heard, they were dating and having a fantastic time.

And my client? He and the waitress got engaged a year after that night. That restaurant *had* been calling me. All of us were supposed to be there at that particular time, all for love.

SIX

———————

Finding out who was invading my body and soul was one thing. Figuring out how to keep ahold of myself was completely different. And this was where I was in uncharted territory.

Ever since I was a child, the dead have come to me. They have showed me their last hours, or the years of abuse, or the people responsible for their deaths. They have told me, in their individual ways, that they are not ready to go. One prankster named Tod would hang around just to make me laugh. He'd worked as a clown before he died of a heart attack in his fifties. He would stop by, eat from the fridge, tell me knock-knock jokes. Finally, I took him with me on one of my trips to New Orleans. I thought Bourbon Street would be a great place for him. I was right. He stayed, and now I see him when I go back to visit the city, mingling in his clown costume alongside the palm readers and dancers in Jackson Square.

Another of my visitors stayed with me for eight years. He appeared a few days after 9/11 and just took up residence. He would shave and get ready for the day and then go down to my office and get to work. I knew it was a residual haunting and that he wasn't ready to face his own death in the Twin Towers. He just kept working, every day like the last. Until one day, a woman—whole and alive—came to see me. She had finally broken from the grief of losing her husband in the terrorist attacks and was close to killing herself. She came to me to find reasons not to. And I, without realizing it at first, had one for her. My friend, who watched many of my work sessions, stared at her in shock. For the first time, he asked me if he had died in the first tower. He knelt before his wife and told her that she was not ready to join him. She did not hear him with her ears, but she did hear him with her heart. He had been working all that time, even in death, to give his family a better life.

But these hauntings and others always left room for me when they visited. They always respected me as a person and gave me my own space. Until Patricia. She really was trying to take over. And it was now to the point where it was really pissing me off. I've always been empathetic toward the dead—obviously—and before this, that had always been an easy and natural way for me to act. I had started my "relationship" with Patricia that way, wanting to help her and solve whatever her problem was. But she wasn't like the others, and she wasn't letting me be my own person. She wasn't helping me figure out what she wanted—she didn't even seem all that interested in my help. She just seemed to want me for my body, literally. She would come at any time, day or night, and I could not stop her. I was losing my ability to control myself.

I knew what was happening, and that made it all the more difficult. She was forcing me aside, taking over. I kept fighting. I liked being me—even with all my baggage. I liked myself, and I wanted to stay. But she kept shoving me away, diminishing my own characteristics and asserting her own chaotic, schizophrenic mind. I thought I might soon go crazy, too. I am completely aware of the signs of possession, and the psychic attacks were becoming too much. Soon, I would be unable to fight back.

I now knew better than to answer a knock on the door, but she found other ways to pull me back to the mental hospital, to the place she had experienced such terror and abandonment. I kept catching glimpses, and then one night, I was suddenly back there again, looking through a small window in a steel door. I saw doctors and nurses passing by outside, not even looking my way. I started yelling that my name was Jackie—insisting that I was still myself. No one listened.

As I paused for breath, I heard the shuffling of many feet and turned around to find ten people behind me. They were all wearing blue-and-white hospital gowns and whispering to themselves. They moved toward me and started pulling and pawing at my hair and scratching at my arms. As I fought them off, I realized I was wearing the same kind of hospital gown. I shoved them away and turned back to the tiny window, screaming for help. I pounded on the steel door, and with every bang, the overhead lights flickered.

I wiped my tears away and saw unfamiliar blue-and-black makeup come off on my hands. I stared at my hands. I didn't see my tattoos. Who was I? I yelled until I was hoarse, and then a sharp spark stopped me. The overhead lights began to sway in different directions. I looked from them back through the little window. The corridor was empty.

I should not have turned around, because now I had to turn back. I slowly spun around and found myself in an empty classroom. The desks were lined up in neat rows, and the ABCs stretched across a dusty blackboard. I heard someone coming behind me and turned back to the little window, which was still there in the steel door. I swallowed hard and thought to myself, *Okay, I'm getting out. Or waking up. Whatever comes first. Just let me go!*

I glanced back at the classroom, which remained empty, and then back to the window. And there he was. The dark figure, with his shy smile and his black, sinister eyes, just inches from me. I jerked back in terror and stumbled into a row of desks, knocking them over. I tensed and stared at the steel door, waiting for it to blow open.

There was a laugh behind me. Again, I had to turn. The tall man in black was writing rapidly on the blackboard, although this time, he had on a white T-shirt. I stayed very still, hoping I would just wake up. He continued writing and then underlined something at the bottom of the board and moved to the side. I saw the words appear slowly.

I am the Zodiac and you are the Fifth Element.

I closed my eyes, praying for escape, but the only thing I got was his breath on my face as he moved right in front of me. He started talking about the Bible, and I tried to block him out with my own words. "This isn't real. This isn't real. My name is Jackie. My name is Jackie." My eyes stayed shut.

"Did you hear me?" a voice roared in my ears. "Were you listening to me?"

I opened my eyes. I sat in my bedroom, slumped on the floor beside my bed. My ears still rang from his shouting. I had heard, loud and clear.

Most folks hear the word *possession* and run. They think one could only be possessed by an evil spirit or entity. Not so. Sometimes it is wearing the skin of another, not necessarily one who was evil. But it buries your own self just the same.

Imagine going into a vintage clothing store and picking up a hat. The color is worn and faded, the fabric is thin, the pattern doesn't quite blend like it used to. It is well worn, and well loved. Try it on. It fits perfectly. Does it bring its past with it?

If an artist had owned it, one might feel the creativity

and passion. If it had been owned by a man of the cloth, one might feel closer to God, protected and blessed. But if it had belonged to the victim of a gruesome crime, what would be hidden in its fabric? A lifetime cut short, a horrible end? No one would ever want such a sensation snug against the head. Such hard luck and torment might follow you. Or what if the residue of the perpetrator remained in the hat, like a worm in the material, until you place it on your head, and it slowly slips into your ear, all warm and comfortable? It begins so slowly. You look around. There's no one in sight, but you are so sure you heard a voice. So don't touch that hat! Just in case your skeptical nature is proven wrong. What would become of you?

I'll tell you if you're willing to listen.

I left the house, quietly, just before dawn. The city was still asleep, and the peacefulness of the streets calmed me as I walked. I wandered, letting my feet take me where they wanted, until they stopped in front of Our Lady of Angels Catholic Church, a few blocks from my house. I stood there, looking at the entrance to the huge brick front of the Catholic church. I did not want to go in. Maybe it was because I felt like I did not belong. Or maybe it was the fear of agitating the demon I was sure resided within me. Just like my mother.

The door clicked and swung open as I stared at it from the sidewalk. The devil's voice came from within. "Jackie, why bother? It's not like you don't know me. It's just a house. That's all it is. I, too, can walk right in. I'm not the sucker that jumped on the cross. I told him. I warned him. Did he listen?

"Walk away, Jackie. Come to me. Look, don't take it so personal. Long before the existence of this world as you know it, we sort of had this meeting. It went like this—if you take Park Place, I get the Boardwalk. Oh, yeah . . . That boardwalk . . . Do you remember the ocean waves?" He was taunting me with my mother's death at the Surf Hotel. He had met me in the water outside. It had been such a long time ago. I would not take his bait.

I looked away from the door and toward the massive stone angel in front of the church. It began to rain. I took my hood off and let the water hit my face as I stood in peace. I felt centered, and I felt that I could do this. I have always believed in God, and I pray often. I pushed open the heavy iron gate and started up the steps. A sharp stabbing pain went through my back, forcing me to grab the railing as my knees buckled.

"God isn't home today! But I'm always ready to extend my hand. Go on, Jackie. They'll only deem you nuts. Schizophrenic. And then no one will have use for you. What will you say?" the devil asked mockingly. " 'The devil made me do it'? It's the insane asylum for you, Jackie, my own private playground. And then we can be the best of friends. Who knows? Maybe your mom will come out and play . . ."

The steps went on forever. I hung on to the railing with both hands as a pain that felt like a thousand bee stings went across my back. My feet stuck in foul-smelling mud and felt heavy as I struggled to lift them.

"Oh, Jackie, I know how to hurt you! It begins with an *M*. Come on, guess. *Bzz!* Your time is up. The word is *mother*. Mother. Mother. She didn't love you, Jackie."

I reached the top of the stairs and straightened my tortured back. A huge wall of fire blocked the door. I still felt the peace of the angel statue. I could do this. I smirked back at the voice and then walked through the fire. It was nothing, just an illusion, gone in an instant. I stood in the church. Light shone through the stained glass and fell on a large crucifix. It was beautiful and godly, and it did not stop him.

"I'm a man with many talents . . . I go by different names. That you already know. I have workers—soldiers of destruction that don't even realize I exist. A simple gesture from me or a flicker of a thought put into their simple minds. That's all it takes and the job is done—and I go on . . . Now, let's cut to the chase. One of my best and, yes, favorite soldiers is missing something. Oh, I was so proud of him. Bringing New York City to its knees, causing my favorite elements—mayhem and chaos."

He switched from boasting about his minion to targeting his quarry.

"She has been hiding, waiting. Getting the prized medium's attention!" He was pleased with that. Pleased that he saw a way into me. "The girl with the gift carries a high price . . . like a bounty. What a trophy you would be. The magic you can spin excites me."

His voice continued to echo through the church. "What do you say we have a meeting of minds . . . You'll get your sanity back, and my masked man stays happy—my soul eater. A fascinating young man, striking. He carried the Bible all day, stalked the streets by night."

He asked if I liked astrology. I braced myself as the ceiling of the church peeled away and stars appeared with lines connecting the signs of the zodiac.

I stumbled to the front of the church, where a golden chalice sat upon a marble altar, and I prayed for God to please be with me. The altar melted away, and in its place stood a table, set for tea. A little girl was serving a cookie to a large man in a mask. As she placed the cookie on his plate, she knocked over the chalice. Blood spilled down the white tablecloth and dripped loudly onto the floor. The masked man pulled her onto his lap.

"How does it feel to have something that doesn't belong to you?"

I screamed so loudly my lungs hurt. "Let her go! Let *me* go!"

His taunts continued over my screams. "No one will believe you," he yelled as I turned to flee. "They'll think you're insane. A schizophrenic." It was my deepest fear—the torment of a fractured mind, the affliction of schizophrenia. I ran.

A gentle tug stopped me. An old man had grasped the sleeve of my sweatshirt and now chided me for running in church. As I turned to tell him that I meant no disrespect, I saw that the tea party was gone. Only the quiet altar and the gleaming chalice remained. I felt like my mind was fracturing right then and there.

The man said he was the church's caretaker and guided me to a pew. He sat next to me, but I stared straight ahead. I didn't know what to say anymore. No one would believe me. Somehow, I had known this day would come.

"I think I'm losing my mind," I whispered to this caretaker. "I'm seeing things and hearing things. They appear, then disappear. I'm becoming something else . . . someone else."

His eyes were so kind. I went on talking, trying to explain it to him and to myself. I had always lived on that fine line that most people didn't know even existed. I could look through a two-way mirror, an ordinary girl born with an extraordinary gift that at any moment could turn into a curse. If I was able to see demons, then they were able to see me. The living dead . . . I lived among them; they communicated with me on every level.

"Do you believe that the devil has an army of living beings—human? Do you believe the dead have a message and that they would go to any length to be heard? Do you believe that these demons can take shape into any form or can pass through from person to person?" I asked. "Well, do you?"

He finally nodded yes, as though we had something in common.

"Through the ages, I have seen structures torn down to a complete wasteland," he said. "Starvation, the sun burning down, spreading fire, destroying everything in its path. Disease, devastation, and poverty. Human beings, cattle—together to be wiped out. The war of the worlds."

He shook his head sadly. "It's disgraceful, just disgraceful." His head stilled. "But I have also seen the power and the mighty. The rise of man. Pandora's box was lifted, shifted, and slammed down. The earth moved once again; the meek stood up in the name of bravery and fought back. So my answer is yes. I do believe!"

He sat back in the pew, staring up at the crucifix as if it were speaking to him—or through him. I stood up and left quietly so I would not disturb his silent moment with God. I stopped at the large doors and looked back to whisper my thanks. As I pushed the doors open, he called to me in his gentle voice.

"Jackie, just one thing. Always stay in the middle of the road." He winked and smiled at me.

"Who are you?" I asked.

"Just a messenger," he said. "You won't know your strength until you face your weakness."

I walked outside as his words repeated in my head. My weakness, my fear. The schizophrenic soul. I was going to have to go in to find my way out.

SEVEN

I stood outside the church, where everything looked normal and sane. But I now knew I was going to have to go somewhere that was neither. Patricia had been pulling me toward her nightmare, and I was done resisting. I hailed a cab and told the driver to take me to the Bellevue psych hospital.

"Did you say you want to go to the old Bellevue ward?" Before I could answer, he ripped into me. "Look, I had a hard night. Punks skipping fares, girls dropping their drawers having sex in the back. Fights, hair weaves being pulled out. It's out of control, and if I don't pick them up, it's called discriminating. It's called bullshit to me. So what is it, lady? Don't think you're going to jump while I'm on the clock. God as my witness, I'll beat the devil right out of you. You got that?"

How I wished he could. But he was just a tired working

stiff at the end of a bad shift. I told him I was just going to see a friend.

He eyed me. "Okay . . . one false move back there, and a can of whoop ass is going to be opened. Yeah, that's right, New York style . . ."

Oh, I did like this guy. He'd seen almost everything—the night crawlers, the drunks, the weirdos, the freaks, and maybe even the ones like me. He wore a small cap tilted to one side and a leather jacket that was probably two sizes too small. He spent the ride gnawing on a smelly unlit cigar stump and giving me the hairy eyeball in his rearview mirror. Finally, he couldn't contain his natural cabbie chatter any longer.

"So, lady, what is it? Guy problems? Nah . . . Why would someone like yourself try to get into that crazy house?"

"Who said I'm trying anything?" I asked back. "I told you, I'm just making a fast visit, sort of collecting something . . ."

He told me that the place was now a homeless shelter for men, which I already knew. Although it was down the street from Bellevue Hospital Center, the famous trauma and research facility, the old psych building wasn't affiliated with it at all. The driver knew the difference and steered the cab toward the right location. Then he introduced himself as Tony and asked my name.

"My name is Jackie." I realized that I had said it in an uncertain tone. I rubbed my hands together, trying my best to stay in full possession of my own body and mind. It was easier right now than it had been; there were no voices pounding in my head, fighting with me. I wondered why Patricia was leaving me alone.

"I'm not trying to be nosy or nothing, but you got a relative up in there?" Tony asked.

"Yeah, I guess you can say that," I said. "I'm just going in to pick something up from someone. Listen, if you wait for me, I'll pay you double—for your time and generosity."

"Look, I don't do this, but I'll wait. I wouldn't want to be you." *No kidding,* I thought as he continued, "Hey, you know, my grandmother from the other side, she used to say, 'If you do good, good comes back.' So I'll wait."

We pulled up along the side of the hulking stone building, and as I got out, Tony warned me not to bring any smelly homeless people back to his cab. This guy really had seen a lot. I steeled myself for what I would have to see before I returned to his taxi and then walked around to the entrance. It was still as bleak and grim as before. And the environment wasn't helped by its neighbor. The New York City Office of Chief Medical Examiner was right across the street. Bellevue's patients—and now the homeless—had nothing but a steady stream of death every time they looked out the windows. And not easy, natural deaths, either. Only the homicides, the suicides, and the unclaimed John Does came by van to that place. Nice view for people who needed help and compassion, wasn't it?

I walked up to the front doors, where two security guards stood. They shooed me away—no women allowed in the men's shelter. I stood back and looked up at the dead vines clinging to the brick, reaching several stories up. I knew which floor was calling me, but how was I going to get there?

My gaze fell on the line of men waiting to get in for the night. Each one was searched before the guards allowed them in—their poor, torn garbage bags rifled through, as if they had no property rights at all. My heart hurt for them. Didn't they have any family who could help them?

Hmmm. I walked back up to the hard-ass guards. "My brother is on the front of the line. I'm here to take him home."

They didn't budge, just tried to stare me down. I told them that his name was Tony, and he was sick and contagious. "Who knows, you probably have it anyway by now."

Their stony glares broke as they nervously asked what my "brother" had.

"Some kind of flesh-eating parasite that spreads like wildfire."

"Shit," said one of them. "Go on ahead and get him out. You got two minutes—in and out, lady."

I darted inside, quickly found a set of stairs, and began to climb two at a time. Syringes and crack vials littered the floor. Mold grew thick on the walls, and there were still psychiatric devices around, like mouthpiece restraints and leather straps.

As I approached the fifth floor, I began to hear noises again. The door from the stairwell had a padded knob that crackled under my fingers as I turned it. I stepped into the corridor and watched it transform back into what it had been. Psychiatric hell.

One at a time, the overhead lights clicked on. Gurneys came out of corners and lined up against the walls. Wheelchairs that had been flung into a pile righted themselves and rolled out into a neat line. Demon Sally yelled at me from the nurses' station.

I felt as though I was out of my body and in a dream as I began walking down the hallway. The floor creaked beneath my feet as I headed for room 7. I peeked through the little glass windows of the rooms I passed on the way. Each held broken human beings huddled in the corners of their private hells.

I got to room 6. I thought I was almost there. Silly me. I heard moaning, but I couldn't see through the little window because it was covered in some fetid gunk. Gagging from the smell, I scanned the floor for something to wipe it away. Trash was everywhere, and I picked up a small piece of paper. It looked like an advertisement of some sort as I unfolded it.

Come one, come all . . .

Big, bold letters began to appear, one by one.

Surf Hotel.

The place where my mother died. The place she was killed by a demon during an exorcism. I fell against the wall, trying to catch my breath. I knew it was a full-blown panic attack, but that knowledge didn't help at all. I was stuck up here, in this hell, and I couldn't breathe.

I tried to sneak past room 6 without it seeing me. This isn't real, I repeated to myself. It can't hurt me anymore. A face that I recognized came to the window, looking wildly from side to side as it tried to find me. It was the demon that had killed my mother.

That was a battle I did not want to fight again. I ran toward room 7 and flung open the door. I could see as I walked in that the window looked out onto the medical examiner's building. The view inside was just as terrible. Sewage dripped from the ceiling. A bloodstained mattress leaned against a wall. A child's desk was tossed in the corner. I moved further in.

Something inside the closet started banging. I tried to ignore it as I saw a yellow wristband on the floor. It had my name on it. I picked it up in horror. In my addled brain, I had become an official psychiatric patient, which was one of my greatest terrors. I had no choice but to put it on. As I fastened it around my arm, the closet door flew open and out came that damn wheelchair again. It rolled forward and waited for me. I knew that this time, I could not avoid the ride. I arranged all of the restraints neatly around the chair and then took my seat.

The only way out was in.

I sat in the wooden wheelchair with a wristband on. The restraints swung free, but I was trapped all the same. The room approved and started to tidy itself. Trash cleared away and the desk righted itself as a fog rolled in. I knew what was coming and began to cry. I knew I was the offering.

The tall man in black stepped out of the cloud. His

zodiac sign glowed white against his black hood. I stared at him as he bent down toward my face. I couldn't move. It was psychic paralysis. I was being invaded by another force, and it completely immobilized me. I have interviewed thousands of people throughout my career who have experienced this—able to see and hear everything yet not allowed to move a muscle. It's a well-known occurrence in parapsychology. But even though I knew exactly what was happening, I was still terrified. He leaned closer, and his breath smelled like rotting flesh and old blood.

"Jackie, you have come home . . ."

I felt a knife plunge into me. I tried to look at my body but couldn't see the wound. Patricia's wound. I was almost completely lost now. Jackie was leaking out through Patricia's wounds.

"I told you to stay dead, didn't I?" His breath reeked. "How many times must I kill you?"

A piece of paper floated through the air and landed in my lap. "Go on, pick it up! Read the paper, Gemini!"

I couldn't move.

The paper was empty, except for the sign of the Gemini, written in blood.

"You see—that's us. Isn't it fun? You can be Patricia and I can be the Zodiac Killer, and we can play . . . We both have company. Our twins!" The Gemini. He flipped back and forth so quickly. One second talking to Jackie and the next to Patricia. Now he switched back, leaning in closer to address Patricia.

"You worthless piece of schizophrenic shit. Coming back . . How dare you mock me!" He paused, and I could feel his sick smile behind the mask. "But I must say I do like the person you picked. The power I could get from her. And my boss is so pleased with your choice."

The smile and the stench made the room start to spin. He leaned in closer still.

"Close your eyes and listen to my voice. . . You will be two . . ."

I did as I was ordered, and the wheelchair threw me forward. I sprawled on the floor and opened my eyes to find myself back in the stairwell. I tripped over piles of trash and broken floor tiles as I ran, as fast as I could, toward the exit. I pushed past the two thug security guards and found Tony. That should show how bad it was getting for me—that my safe haven was a New York taxi cab. We pulled away, and I begged him to drive me back home. He turned to look at me and pointed to my wrist. "What's that yellow bracelet? You're wearing a hospital band?"

I pulled at it frantically until it came off. It was all real, and I was in real trouble. I stuffed it in the pocket of my sweatshirt and curled up in the backseat. I guess I looked so bad that tough-guy Tony took pity on me and shook off my money.

"Today's your lucky day. Keep it." He handed me his business card and eyed me carefully. "Hey, take this in case you need a private ride to hell again."

Thanks, Tony, but I was already there.

EIGHT

Patricia's presence was becoming so intense, I found myself deliberately planning ways to elude her. One day, on the way to the dentist—that's how desperate I was for some normalcy—I thought I'd try the farmers' market. I got off at the Fourteenth Street–Union Square station so I could walk through the stalls and lose myself in the crush of people.

This was what I loved about New York. Give us a space, and we'll make it happen. You could buy almost any kind of fruit or vegetable in that stretch. People jostled one another as they reached for the best fruit. Vegetables clanged onto scales as growers weighed their sales. Somewhere nearby, I could smell that someone was selling delicious apple-cider donuts. It was all packed together, tickling every one of my senses and making me feel safe.

I stopped at an apple stand, with half a dozen varieties piled high. I picked them up, one by one, enjoying the feeling of the fruit in my hands as I looked for the perfect apple to buy. The conversation of two women nearby washed over me. They were talking about work, and I smiled to myself. Ordinary life. One of the women looked over at me, and as she took a bite of her own apple, her companion's words and my surroundings started to fade away from me. I grabbed my head but couldn't look away from the woman, whose apple was covered in writhing maggots. Her features turned sharp and frightening as she laughed and licked at her disgusting corpse-delight snack.

My stomach heaved, and I threw up, right in front of the apple cart. When I straightened, there were no maggots; there was no evil. Just people staring at a sick woman who had fouled the farmers' market. I staggered away and slowly made my way to the dentist's office. I no longer felt safe. Even worse, I was starting to feel crazy. I did not know what to do.

Somehow, I made it to the big building in Midtown, where Rick, the doorman, greeted me by name, as usual. I came to my dentist pretty often. I confess that I'm addicted to teeth whitening. So everybody in the office, and Rick in the lobby, knew me quite well. It was a beautiful lobby, and interesting. It had two elevators—one big and one small. The small one was a tiny box that seemed to get smaller once you stepped inside. I hate cramped spaces. So, naturally, that was the elevator I got. I reluctantly stepped inside and sweated as I counted the chime for each passing floor. I finally reached the eighth floor, stepped out, and stopped short. My dentist's office should have been to the left in the hallway, just as it had been for years. But this hallway was covered with sheets of plastic and looked like it was under construction.

"Hello?" I called loudly. The plastic sheeting blew and snapped against itself, so at first I didn't hear the shuffling. It slowly took on the sound of a child's feet and then I heard a child's laugh. On the other side of the plastic, as if through a fog, I saw a little girl dressed in a yellow raincoat. She was skipping along slowly, chanting a nursery rhyme, and holding a red ball under her arm. I quietly parted the plastic to get a better look without her seeing me. I watched her hop along, clutching the ball with one hand and, under her other arm, a teddy bear. She couldn't have been more than seven or eight years old. She turned as though someone called to her, and I saw a man walking toward her. I could only see the back of his dark green uniform as he bent down toward her. I tried to walk forward to stop him but couldn't move.

"Don't be afraid," he said, caressing her soft curls. "Do you like puppy dogs or kittens?" he asked. "I have lots of them. I spoke to your mommy, and she said you're such a good girl I could give you one."

"You spoke to my mommy?" she said, in that pure child's voice.

"Yes, I sure did." He pinched her cheek, trying his damnedest to gain her trust. Easy to do with such innocence. He told her to leave her toys. She would need to carry her new pet instead. He would come back for her toys later. "Promise . . . Cross my heart."

She dropped her ball and teddy bear and took his hand. I know how these things end, but I refused to let this one turn out that way. Not on my watch. I wrenched myself away from the wall and flung myself toward them. They didn't hear or see me, and I ran right through them both. I stumbled and fell face-first into the opposite wall. I spun around and saw her toys, but the two of them were gone.

"God damn it! Where did you go?" I shouted as I ran down the hallway. "Give her back . . . Give me that child!"

The elevator doors were banging open and shut so fast I couldn't get on. I ran toward the emergency stairwell and a shadow loomed behind the plastic closest to the door. It was the tall man in black. He spoke through the plastic.

"You can't stop the process . . . We, too, have a purpose. I will eat your sins and take your soul . . ."

I ran past, pushed the exit door open, and took the stairs down two at a time. I did not slow until the fourth floor, when I heard a woman's singing. I rounded the turn in the stairs and saw a large broken mirror on the wall. In front of it was that Patricia woman. I edged past her, hoping she wouldn't notice me as she stared at her own reflection. She didn't, and after I made it past, I turned to look. She was the one haunting me, after all—I didn't feel too bad about invading her privacy.

She stood in front of the mirror, fixing her lipstick, swaying her sultry body back and forth, making eyes at herself. She told herself that she was pretty and dabbed at her heavily made-up face, like she was getting ready to go search the night for some good-looking taker. I quietly backed away and ran faster than ever down the remaining steps and into the lobby.

Rick, the doorman, rushed over and grabbed my arms.

I must have looked absolutely nuts as I babbled about a child getting taken and a woman in the stairwell and an entire floor of the building under construction.

"Jackie, calm down," he said, still holding my arms. "You've been up there for more than twenty-five minutes."

I hauled him into the elevator and pushed for the eighth floor. I had to prove myself to him. I had to prove myself— to me. The damn box finally chimed for the eighth floor, and the doors slid open. Rick, like the gentleman he was, held it open so I could go first.

"Just drop the bullshit," I snapped. "You go first."

He walked out, looked around, and then spread his arms wide, as if to say, "See, not a thing out of place." I slowly walked out of the elevator and looked around. I ran my hands along the walls for traces of plaster and work dust. Nothing. I swung open the utility-room door near the stairwell. Nothing but a broom.

"Why are you doing this?" I asked Rick.

He looked at me. He had known me for years. "Jackie, are you working on a homicide?"

"No," I snapped again. "And if I was, what does that have to do with it? You think I've gone mad, don't you?"

He hesitated. "No. I think you saw something real bad. Real bad. I'm getting creeped out!"

"Yeah, me, too," I said as I yanked open the door to my dentist's office.

"Jackie!" said the smiling receptionist. "Where did you go? We were looking all over for you."

I stared at her in astonishment.

"You came in, sat down, and then just got up as though you were sleepwalking," she continued. "I went out in the hallway—you were gone."

I told her I would reschedule my appointment and walked out. Rick waited with me for the elevator.

"Hey, Jackie," he said softly, "I believe you."

It didn't matter. I rode down to the lobby without saying a word. I needed help.

Joanne was waiting for me in the lobby. My wonderful, beautiful grown daughter, who I always met with for lunch after my dentist appointments. I would get her all to myself for the rest of the day, and we would catch up on everything. It was one of our traditions. I had been so excited about it today. Before all of that had happened.

"Hey! You ready for our date?" She came over and kissed me on the cheek and then drew back. "You look awful. Did you have work done, or just a cleaning?"

I dragged her out of the building before I started talking. We walked and I talked. I confided everything. The woman who was following me everywhere. The man with the mask. The little girl. How did they all connect? What did they want from me?

We found a café and ordered coffee. I described every detail I could remember. Joanne held my hand and listened until something I said triggered a memory and she spoke. The tall man in black with the slicked-back hair and the thin ponytail had come to our home a week earlier, she said. She had been working on my schedule when there was a knock on the door. When she'd answered it, a man fitting that description had handed her a sealed envelope and said it was for me.

I yanked my hand away and stared at her in horror.

"I told you—never get the door! Don't you ever listen? For the love of God, we work not only with the dead, but the ones who took their lives, too. These criminals know who we are! Don't you understand the danger? Get smart, girl!"

She grabbed my hand back. "People are looking!"

"I don't give a shit who hears me," I yelled. "It could be your life!"

I tried to collect myself. I made her promise not to tell Will anything about it. I didn't want him worried.

Joanne glared at me. "For Chrissakes, Mom, we're all worried. You're on the streets at night. You lock yourself away and don't talk to anyone!" Now she was the one yelling. "And what's the sudden change in the way you're dressing and that . . . What's that you're wearing? And where in God's name did you get that color lipstick? Who are you dealing with? I'm your partner in work. I have a right to know!"

I stood up and threw enough money on the table to cover our bill and our disruption of the quiet café. All I could think about was going home and finding that envelope. We rushed back together and began to tear apart my office, full of questions and fear. We sat on the floor of that room for hours, going through every file and looking at every stack of paper. We could not find the envelope.

As we ransacked my office, I began to think that there might not be any envelope at all. Maybe the whole thing had been a psychic vision seen by only Joanne. She had never been plagued with visions of demons like I had, thank God, but she did have the gift of sight.

When Joanne was four years old, her favorite story was one she'd made up about a long road in the California desert. She had never been to California, but she loved this road and once drew me a picture of her imaginings. It had a gas station and a tiny diner that she labeled "Little Jake's." Fifteen years later, Will and I took a vacation to the coast and rented a fast little convertible—it was California, after all—and then promptly got lost. We ended up out in the desert and stopped to ask directions at a roadside diner. We got the directions, and a couple of slices of the best pie I'd ever tasted. As we sat in our rented car and savored the pie, I looked up at the diner's sign. Little Jake's. Just like Joanne had drawn so many years before.

As she got older, Joanne began to realize that she and I were different from other folks. Another one of her pictures illustrated this. It was a whole menagerie of people—different colors and ages—all standing in and around a crooked country house. I asked her who all those people were. All of seven years old, she took me through every single one. Some lived with us—in the walls or under the beds. Some were standing outside waiting to get in, and some were inside, wanting to get out. As she sat in my lap and explained her artwork, I looked across the front yard and could see her drawing materializing.

She pointed, because she saw it, too. "Why can't we be like other people?" she asked. I knew exactly what she meant, and I knew she needed the truth. "We can't be anything we aren't," I had said.

"I've got it!" Joanne yelled now, startling me out of my memories as I sat next to her on the office floor. I thought she'd found the envelope, but instead she started shouting about the security system and the camera right outside the front door. We both leaped to our feet and ran for the monitors. I couldn't believe we hadn't thought of it before.

We queued up the footage and began to watch the recording from that day. We saw several comings and goings—the mailman, delivery drivers, acquaintances, even people just strolling by the house and pointing. It's not like I live in witness protection. People know who I am, and are always curious.

Finally, we found it. It showed Joanne coming to the door, talking through the intercom, and then opening the door. I looked at the screen and then at her without saying a word. I guess the look on my face spoke for me.

"This is all because of you," she snapped. "Telling me they always find us! Now I'm scared!"

I turned back to the monitor, which showed Joanne at the door, talking to no one. She reached out her hand and seemed to take something, although there was nothing there. She even looked down at her empty hand, exactly as if she were examining an envelope someone had just given her. Her days were long and full of work and her busy personal life. She had no reason to make this up, no reason to put on a show for me. And she hadn't. At the very end of her encounter at the door, I saw something on the recording. It was very slight—just a movement of air, a shift in the atmosphere, as though the breeze had for a split second twirled like a tiny tornado. It was one of those things the normal eye wouldn't see. Couldn't see. But I could.

Everything was starting to make sense to me, and it was very frightening. I saw Joanne communicating with a powerful force who was able to appear only to her. Was it an earthbound evil spirit? Was it just a person who had passed on? Was it a demon trying to infect and infest? I had to figure it out to combat it. If it was the same man in black who had been stalking me, it was now trying to broaden its hunt to include my child. And I would not allow that to happen.

NINE

———————

Joanne and I kept working in the months that fol-
lowed, even though it was more and more difficult for me
to push Patricia aside. But my clients needed me. One day,
a beautiful woman in her thirties called and begged
Joanne for an immediate appointment. She had seen me
many times before with issues related to buying and selling property and other times just to help keep herself on
a spiritual path. She seemed to be in great distress, so
Joanne squeezed her into my schedule.

This lady had been living with her boyfriend for years,
and they had been completely happy. But now her parents
were pressuring her to get married. I, as usual, have defi-
nite opinions about that. I say, if it ain't broke, don't fix
it. Marriage can destroy relationships—I've seen it happen
many times. That one piece of paper can change people
and make them think they need to fill a role outside of
just making sure the other person is happy. Marriage

doesn't necessarily keep people faithful or keep them from being lonely. It's all about what works for the individual couple.

So my pretty lady comes to see me. She was absolutely frantic, which was completely out of character for her. We got her some water and laid her down on the couch in my office. I noticed perspiration on her bare feet as I sat in a chair next to her and waited for her to speak. She told me she was possessed and needed an exorcism. No sooner had she gotten the words out than she started thrashing around and babbling.

Now I admit this looked like some wild shit. It was possible the devil could have snuck in without me noticing, but highly unlikely—especially in a client I knew well. I concentrated as she convulsed on my couch. There was no demon there.

"What is this? Stop that head shaking! You're going to work up a good headache, not to mention break my prized couch," I said. "Enough!"

She kept at it, growling and crying. I went into the bathroom, reached into the toilet, and scooped out a handful of water. I returned to the office and threw it right in her face. She arched her back and screamed that it was burning her. I wiped my hands on her dress and sat back down.

"Hey, sweets, that wasn't holy water," I said. She opened one eye and peeked at me. "That was toilet water, and the bowl hasn't been cleaned in a good week."

She sat up and wiped her face off. "Yuck, Jackie, that's gross."

"Yup, it is," I said.

She stared at me and sighed. Then she explained. Her mother wanted her to get married and was laying on the guilt about it. She thought that if she was "possessed," it would give her parents something else to focus on and worry about, and they would lay off the marriage pressure. She couldn't just tell her mother how she felt.

I shook my head. The things that people come up with. But now it was my turn. "You scrub the bowl and wash the bathroom floor," I told her. That was the penalty for trying to pull a fast one on me. "And I'm calling your mother." That was so I could sort out this mess.

I got the lady on the phone and explained who I was and that her daughter was so worried about disappointing her parents that she would rather act like she was possessed by a demon. Her mother kept asking if the whole thing was some kind of joke. "Nope. I got your daughter right next to me. She can call you back after the bathroom is clean," I said.

I ended the conversation and waited for my client to finish her scrubbing. "So, what's up?" I asked with gentle amusement in my voice. "Did you see *The Exorcist*?"

She got a sheepish look on her face. "Yeah, it was on last night."

I gave her the phone and listened to her talk to her mother. They laughed and cried, and her mother turned out to be very understanding. Except about the demon possession. "Why would you say you were possessed? How awful! You're going to church every Sunday with me. You need God!" her mother said.

My client hung up the phone and looked at me. As I walked her out, I gave her a hug.

"Go to church, girl," I said, "and leave the devil alone."

I burst out of the drugstore, letting the door go so that it almost hit Will as he followed me outside. Let him get his own damn door. I was sick of his questions. Tired of him telling me he no longer recognized me. Sick of—

The store alarm beeped as I stepped over the threshold, piercing my mental tirade. It certainly didn't shut Will up, though.

"Did you—or whoever is living in you—steal something?" he yelled at me.

I turned on him with such anger. "Get off my shit, Will. There isn't anyone in me. Maybe it's you. Or maybe I should just be alone. I'm warning you, Will. Don't push me. I don't shoplift."

I closed in on him as this thing inside of me emerged. I could tell she was defending me from him, but she also was shoving me aside, coming forward in an uncontrollable rage. I couldn't stop her.

"Don't you ever push her around." I kept at him, poking against his chest, this massive six-foot-two bodybuilder with a chest like a rock. I had no trouble backing him up. But the strength was not mine. "Who the fuck needs you?"

With the small shred of me that was left, I knew that if he started to react negatively, it would get dangerous for both of us. Somehow, my beloved man sensed the same thing. He gently pulled me into him as he whispered in my ear. "It's okay. You're okay, Jackie. I love you. Just listen to my voice. Don't let go of yourself . . ."

He took my hand and softly said that he was going to take me home. I felt tears running down my cheeks as our hands locked tightly. "Please don't let this take me," I managed to say.

"Never." He started to lead me home. "You're mine forever, Jackie."

As we walked down the peaceful leafy side streets, the other woman inside me began to relax. I could feel her slowly start to slip aside, as though Will's tender heart and whatever meager strength I had left had been able to subdue her for the moment. Maybe she'd felt our love for each other and had run away. Maybe she'd seen something she'd never had for herself. Maybe she had some unfinished business . . .

These thoughts rattled around in my head as we walked the few blocks home. I went inside and sat down on the couch. I knew I owed him an explanation, but I didn't have one.

"I know it isn't easy for you," he said as he sat beside me, his tone clearly communicating that it wasn't easy for him, either. "I don't know where you go. You don't answer your phone. I feel like I'm dealing with a stranger sometimes. Tell me, Jackie, if you're working on something."

"Something is happening to me," I said slowly. "I look in the mirror and see this woman standing beside me. She lives in me. She follows me . . . I'm scared that one day we are going to switch places. I'll be lost in her dimension, and she'll be living my life with my family . . ."

Had my work done this to me? I had kept all of my clients throughout this whole ordeal, but it was getting more and more difficult to concentrate on them. Did the more I interacted with the other side—the dead— mean that I slipped further into that side? Had part of myself been left behind? Maybe the underworld was fighting over the half of me I had managed to keep. Maybe the devil was competing to win the whole of me. Maybe I was like my mother, a prize he would win.

I buried my head in my hands, but I couldn't block out Will's words.

"On these long night strolls, where do you go? Your feet are covered in dirt in the morning. Look at the sheets! Do I have to start following you?"

He had every right to ask for answers. I had none, but there was something . . . I went into our bedroom, with its Southern Gothic furniture and my beloved painting of the wolf whose spirit protects me, and pulled everything out of my closet. There, in the back, was my journal.

This was my very first journal—I had never kept one before. Some people keep diaries or journals and pour out their deepest thoughts and fears. Not me. I had always been afraid that if I wrote down things that I had felt or experienced—as opposed to writing down the thoughts of the dead who speak through me—and someone found it, they would find the key to things that needed to stay in hell. Some things did not need to be written down. Some secrets you need to hide. The dark images in my mind, the thoughts I could never escape—I always carefully tucked all of these things into the most inaccessible parts of my mind. I kept them away from the dangerously curious. Writing them down would have made them easier for others to find, and to use. It was safer to keep them buried. I knew this better than anyone.

I slid down to the floor, and Will joined me. Fear came over his face as I opened the pages.

I'm writing this to my family. I'm becoming a victim. My days are full, and my nights, I stalk. I've been pulled back into a time I don't remember. I'm living a life that isn't mine . . .

I flipped through the journal, showing Will drawings I had done of a masked man and other pages that were ripped and shredded—Patricia's doing, not mine. Pages written as if by a child, with drawings in red crayon. There was one of a red ball and another of the little girl, who would often visit me, and a man taking her.

Will closed the book, and I put it back in the depths of the closet, like I was hiding it from myself.

"Send her back, Jackie. I'll help you."

Something inside me fell into place, something I think I had really been hiding from myself. In my desperation to get rid of this woman, I had not seen it. But now it clicked, like the snap of a lamp being turned on in the dark.

"I can't," I said slowly, as the light began to penetrate just a little into my black-as-night brain. "If she doesn't complete her task, I will become her . . . She's showing me something . . . while something else is hunting her like an animal . . ."

If I could just stay in my full body and mind, I could figure it out. If only I could . . . The phone in the kitchen rang and jolted me up from my seat on the floor. I was heading for it when Will yelled, "You can't run from me, Jackie." I looked back in surprise—why would he say that?—and where Will had been was the tall man in black.

I bolted into the kitchen and went straight for my trusty knife. With it in one hand, I ripped the phone off the hook with the other. The caller ID said it was Will's cell phone. I whispered into the receiver, "He's in the house. Please help me."

"Call the cops. I'm on my way."

I fumbled with the phone and dropped it as I turned. The tall man in black stood in the kitchen doorway, turning from the vague hologram I sometimes see into a solid mass of a human being.

"Jackie, why aren't you playing nice? Put the knife down before it goes into you a hundred times over."

He gripped the edges of the door frame and then sprang toward me, like a snake uncoiling.

"Thank you for sharing your little drawings and haunting journal with me. We have no secrets, Jackie." He was behind me now, so close I could feel his body, his breath, his voice. I could smell the rot. "You're brave, but I'm the punisher. No one will believe you, Jackie. You're acting irrational. And anyway, I'm in prison. Yep, now you know my secret. Who am I, Jackie?

"I can come and go. I am the grim of the night. You're

learning from the best." He pulled me by my hair back toward him. "I want my soul back . . ."

The door burst open and the alarm went off as Will ran in, knocking things over in his rush to get the intruder. But there was no longer anyone behind me. I threw the knife into the sink—dangerous in my crazy hands—and listened as Will explained that after he told me he was going to start following me, I had gone berserk. He'd needed some time alone, so he had gotten our muddy bedding and taken it to the Laundromat.

I stood at my kitchen sink with the smell of rot still in my nose as my wonderful, protective husband kept running around, trying to find something that was impossible to catch, something that slid in and out of a portal, something that transported itself anywhere and forced me into the depths of hell.

But this time I emerged with more than just fear and confusion. I had managed to find two small rays of light in the darkness. He was in prison, and he wanted a soul returned. Whose soul? His soul, or someone else's? It wasn't much to go on, but it was a start.

This time, I knew I was dreaming. Because I had dreamed of this before. It was the little girl with a raincoat, the one who always seemed to be trying to lead me somewhere in my dreams. But I could never figure out where.

I had seen her—off and on—for most of my life. It was like she was a memory and a ghost all at once. And I knew she would appear again this time because the short man shrouded in mist had come for me. Even though he always escorted me through these dreams, I had never been able to see him completely. I did know that he meant me no harm and would guide me where I needed to go and show me what I needed to see. It was as though you were not allowed to see your angel while you were still among the living.

Tonight, he took me to a building. I never completely saw the structure or the people we passed on the way. It was all like a badly edited movie, jumping from image to image too quickly with a jerking camera. We went inside and walked down a long, sterile hallway. We stopped in front of a large window and I saw little bassinets lined up in rows, with tiny babies tucked snugly inside. Earth's new arrivals.

In all those rows, one name tag stood out. It dangled from a pink ribbon at the end of a bassinet. *Baby Jane.* She lay still. I looked across the glass cubicle of a room and saw what must be her parents, cooing at their precious bundle with adoring looks. The mysterious man next to me brought his hand out from beneath his robe and took mine. He squeezed it, and I felt his sorrow.

Then he let go. I closed my eyes and saw through the child. I saw through her eyes and looked out and above the bassinet at my new parents. I was Jane.

I did not remember every part of her very short life as I lay there in the hospital nursery. It was like flipping quickly through a book, skipping pages everywhere. I was not getting the full story. I was only rushing toward the end. Isn't a book supposed to have a beginning, a middle, and an ending? This one didn't. I went from that nursery straight to my eighth birthday. And then—nothing.

I stumbled out of bed and grabbed for my recorder. I had to get down the raincoat-girl dream that had awoken me. I felt that I might be getting closer to figuring out what she wanted, but my head was literally so crowded with people that my normal intuitiveness had dulled—a once-sharp record needle forced to skip all over, slamming down in a different spot every time.

I finished my recording and drew a bath. I slid my numb body into the hot water and let the scent of the lavender bubble bath soothe me. My eyelids began to feel heavy, and I started to relax. I scooped up a handful of bubbles and stared peacefully at the glistening circles. My head nodded forward.

Suddenly, a cackle filled the air and bubbles flew everywhere. And Patricia was there, sitting at the side of my tub. I sat up quickly and pulled my knees to my chest. As if that made me less vulnerable. Ha.

"You, Jackie, you don't know how to have fun," she said as she grabbed a big bath sponge and began to scrub my back. "Look at how dirty you are . . ." Her scouring made my skin burn. I tried not to gag at the stench of dried blood and the sight of her cracked and gray hands. I did not want to talk to her. I kept my head down, letting only my eyes wander. My gaze fell on my razor, perched on the edge of the tub. God. I reached for it, but she beat me to it.

"Did you ever cut yourself?" she asked. Her eyes were glued to the razor. "Well, did you?"

Enough. I ordered her to give it to me, but she pulled away like a child with a snatched treat. "Come and get it. Catch me!"

She ran right through the door, her laughter the only thing left in the room. I jumped out of the tub, threw my clothes on, and ran after her. I searched every closet and corner of my house, but I couldn't find her or my razor. Still soaked through from the bath, I sat down in my living room. I was insane. No, I was haunted. *Haunted* was the right word. It had to be. My back burned from her heavy hand. I fought back tears.

"Damn you," I screamed. "You rubbed my skin off."

I had tried so hard to be empathetic to her. I had tried asking her what she wanted. I had tried to help her like I had so many other dead souls. But this was the last straw. She was hurting me mentally, emotionally, psychically—and now physically. I was done being nice. I wanted her gone. I don't know how long I sat there, drenched in my own misery, before the phone rang and jolted me out of my daze. It was my mortgage company, wanting to know why my statements were getting returned and my bills weren't paid. *What?*

"Well, your statements are coming back to us—marked up, scribbled on in big, bold letters: MOVED."

I could not come up with an explanation that sounded

at all sensible, so I just went into my office, got my check-book out, apologized, and paid the bill. The late fees and the pay-by-phone charges hurt almost as much as the skin on my back still did. But the woman did realize that my confusion came from the fact that I wasn't responsible for the returned mail.

"I suggest you stop whoever's doing this," she advised.

"Lady, if I could, I would," I said.

She went back to her script and asked if she had been helpful. I was about to brush her off when something occurred to me.

"Oh," I said. "Can I ask you what the name says on the statement envelope?"

Papers rustled on the other end of the line.

"Well, your name was crossed out, stating that you moved. And the only name written is a first name. It just says, 'Patricia.'"

Patricia.

I ended the call and dropped the phone on my desk. Since I was there, I looked around, taking stock of every-thing, including the pile of mail. I rifled through it, not purposefully looking for anything in particular, and I came to one, already opened. I did not remember seeing it before. Or the sender's name.

The return address read:

Heriberto Seda
Great Meadow Correctional Facility
P.O. Box 51
Comstock, NY 12821

I drew a single piece of paper out of the envelope and unfolded it. There was a traced drawing—the outline of his hand.

Dear Jackie

Place your hand in mine if you dear [sic]
Let me show you what lives inside of me
You can't save what is already dead!

Your friend, Eddie

Next to the hand was the simple sign of the Gemini, and below it his signature—and the sign of the zodiac.

TEN

As I looked at the handwriting of Patricia's killer, it gradually came back to me. What she had done. She had really, truly shoved me aside. She had used my hands to write letters to this man. She had reached out, from beyond the grave, to Eddie Seda, the man sitting in prison for her murder.

Slowly, all the missing chunks of time that I'd experienced over almost a year began to come back to me. I hadn't remembered anything at all about my "blackouts" as they were happening, but now they started to become clear. I would be in my own body, fully aware of what I was doing, and then—that fast—I would be standing outside myself, watching a person who looked just like me but wasn't. My mouth would be moving, but the me standing outside couldn't grasp the words. The action was jerky and fast, and I couldn't see or understand anything clearly. It was like an old black-and-white movie, where the film is spliced and jumps forward, and scratchy white lines run through everything.

I now remembered watching myself write letters to Eddie—seeing Patricia looking for answers, trying to finally understand why he had killed her. Her life had never been validated and her death never truly noted. No one had cared. And so her anger and frustration had been building all these years. She was so powerful now.

One occasion came back to me full force. I had been fully within myself and getting ready for the day. I'd moved quietly because the rest of the house was still asleep. I started the shower and tossed my day's clothes on the floor as I searched through my dozens of body washes for what I felt like that morning. I found a honey scrub—perfect—and put it on the side of the tub. I was about to pull my T-shirt and pajama pants off when all the lights dimmed. I began to shake and my breath came fast. I felt like I was trapped. I heard myself call out to Will, and my voice sounded like a faraway echo. I thought I had passed out and hit my head and that I'd dreamed the events that followed. Now I knew I had not.

I walked out of the bathroom and went into my closet, knowing right where to put my hands. Back behind a cabinet, I found three envelopes, stamped and sealed. I didn't look at the names or addresses, just took them and walked out the front door.

I walked down the avenue in my pajamas. I didn't feel the cold. I didn't even feel my feet touch the ground—not once. I looked straight ahead and did not acknowledge anyone I passed. I walked down a long city block and across the avenue to the mailbox. I kissed the letters in my hand, closed my eyes, and tossed them in.

I came back by the same route, not bothering to stop for the two-way traffic. Horns blew and people yelled, but I didn't care. I walked through the front door, which I'd left wide open, and back up to my bedroom. And then I returned to myself. My stomach was heaving, and a horrible, foul odor seemed to be oozing from my pores. The steam from the shower I had left running now filled the whole bedroom. I could barely make out Will, still asleep in bed. I went over to wake him up, and just as my hands moved to shake him, I noticed that he was flat on his back, pressed down into the bed.

I have seen him through the years being held down in his sleep. Thousands of others have come to me and shared these same experiences with me. It's as though a heavy weight is sitting on you, paralyzing you. You are being tormented in your most vulnerable state—sleep. I have seen Will and many others struggle with such entities while sleeping.

I climbed into the bed to help him and clapped my hand over my mouth in horror. He was clacking his teeth together again and again, with enormous force. I shook him and called his name, but he would not wake up. Joanne rushed in and asked what was going on. I told her I had just taken a shower—honestly, that's what I thought I had done—and came out to find him like this. She stepped back from the bed like I was some monster.

"What's that smell?" she demanded. Still busy shaking Will, I did not answer. She stomped into my bathroom, turned off the shower, and came out with the clean clothes I had not changed into. "I thought you said you took a shower." Her tone accused me of lying. I was about to respond when Will came to. The poor man sucked in air like he'd been drowning and then grabbed my arm. His voice was weak and raspy when he finally spoke.

He had seen me go into the bathroom and then heard a struggle. It had sounded like I was fighting with myself. My voice had taken on different tones as I had cursed and screamed. I didn't remember any of that, just blacking out and having that awful dream about walking around on the street outside.

Joanne came over and hugged us both and then wrinkled her nose. The stench was still overpowering. As one, we all looked down at my feet. They were covered in muddy water and dog mess. The poop had stuck between my toes and covered parts of the tattoo on my foot. And now I had gotten it all over the bed as I'd tried to wake up Will.

The vomit came up so fast that I clamped my hand over my mouth to stop it and ran to the bathroom. Will jumped up, too, but couldn't get the toilet seat up in time. The vomit burst through my fingers like water through a dam. Will took charge as I staggered around—grabbing a towel, instructing Joanne to bag the bed sheets and throw them out, and helping me into the shower.

I used the whole bottle of honey scrub, trying to get every last particle of poop off me. When I finally emerged in clean clothes, Will was waiting for me, and he told me more about what had happened to him earlier that morning. He said he saw me go in to take a shower, and he was starting to get up so he could fix me a cup of coffee when a huge dark form appeared and threw him down. He hadn't seen any of this thing's face except the eyes, dark and glassy with a crazed look. The thing pinned him to the bed and started choking him.

"Jackie, this thing was strong. The force was unbelievable. I couldn't move for shit." And this was coming from my Will, whose favorite pastime is working out. And he had felt himself getting pushed down into the bed and the mattress coming up on both sides like he was a human hotdog in a bun. I saw the marks around his neck as he spoke. "That thing kept me down and away from helping you, stopping you from going out the door, no shoes."

I did not know what to say, because I did not know what was going on. I still felt sure I'd blacked out and been dreaming. Just like many other times that I was just now remembering, when I followed my body as it did Patricia's bidding—talking on the phone or writing Eddie to ask for a lock of his hair. Once, I watched myself go down the steps into the garage and hide a bundle of letters. Hide them from myself. Patricia was covering her tracks. She did not want me to know that she was forcing me to communicate with her killer. But now, I had figured it out.

Will was leaving for work. I stood at the glass doors to the garden. I could feel Patricia right behind me. I wanted to spend time with my husband, but at the same time, I couldn't wait to be alone. I longed for those moments when I could roam freely. I knew she was coming faster than ever as I watched him straighten his clothes and give me that smile. The garden behind him began to wilt and die. I felt a single tear fall from my eye. He wiped it away and told me that he didn't have to go in. I said no, that I was fine, and I held him tightly. I squeezed my eyes shut in relief that I could still feel what was closest to me—his heart, as it beat in his chest.

He turned and went down the walkway. I stood at the glass doors and waited for him to turn and wave as he always did. The garden was alive and well now, but the minute he left it, the colors bled away, and weeds choked the life out of everything. I backed away from the glass, feeling inexplicably that I had a task to do. I walked over to the phone, my heart aflutter like I was expecting a call from a long-lost love.

The lights began to flicker, and the whole house began to settle into a tight cube. There were no doors or windows. I started to feel claustrophobic. The phone rang just as I reached for it. The caller ID said "unknown." I picked it up anyway. The person on the other end of the line said my name.

"Who are you?" I asked.

"It's been lonely. I'm cold and scared." She sounded like a child. Her voice crackled and gagged at times, as though she were choking on something. "I'm stuck, just like you, Jackie. I've been trying to get you to help me. You can help me, Jackie. My life is in pieces."

And then she asked me the question so many of them do. "Jackie, am I dead? I come and go in different parts of my life. If I turn one way, I'm doing something completely different. If I turn the other, I'm somewhere else. I can see people, but they can't see me. I can put my hands through things. I can scream and yell and no one turns around but you."

I clutched the phone to my ear and leaned against the counter.

"I have a memory of being pulled out of a cold steel slab. It looks like a tiny freezer, like a tomb. I was in there and then it gets all mixed up. I don't remember eating or sleeping anymore. I don't think I have to do those things anymore.

"Was I that lady in that tiny freezer box all cut open? Tell me, Jackie, tell me."

My throat felt tight, and I couldn't speak. Finally I got my mouth open enough to yell, "Stop it! Why are you doing this to me?"

"I want to know what happened to me. Where am I?" she pleaded. "You are the only one who can see me, help me. It's been so long; I must be missed. Jackie, make the pain stop."

I opened my eyes. I was standing in my kitchen with nothing in my hands. The phone was in its cradle on the wall. I really was losing my mind. And then the phone rang. For real. The number came up on the caller ID. Great Meadow Correctional Facility. No way. I was not picking that up. I turned away.

A voice that was not mine came out of me like a burst of thunder. My head swung to the left and my arm extended as though I were fighting with someone. I swung from side to side as the phone kept ringing. I was shoved against the counter. Pain from the blow stretched up my back and into my neck.

"Don't you walk away from me," the voice that was not mine said. "Pick it up, Jackie. Pick up the phone. I waited so long. Now it's my turn."

Shaking, I picked up the receiver. A recording came on that asked if I would accept the charges for a call from—and then his voice came on the line and I heard him say his name for the first time. Heriberto Seda.

I said I would accept the charges.

"Hello, Jackie," he said over the phone from prison. "How are we doing?"

"We?" I said slowly. "Who's *we*, Eddie?" I was sweating and freezing at the same time. Patricia didn't care. She started talking to him through me.

He began to chuckle. "Oh, there you are," he told Patricia. "I thought I'd lost you."

She screamed at him. "You can't get me. You're locked up!"

"Oh, you're so wrong, Patricia. We are all in. Jackie, I want you to listen to me—" Patricia kept screaming, not wanting to hear his words. She insisted, over and over, that she had been loved and he had taken everything.

"I was loved. You took my life, you son of a bitch." The screaming was unbearable. My ears felt like they were shattering. I slipped down to the floor, unable to let go of the phone.

Eddie broke through her wailing. "If you're done

now," he said to her and then focused on me. "Jackie, I want her back."

Patricia's voice responded. "No! I trusted you. I followed you. I just wanted you to give me a kiss and a cigarette. What did you do to me? You didn't even know my name!"

Eddie was unfazed on the other end of the phone. "Of course I did. Don't you remember, Patricia? You told me your name. You're my companion. You can't run. Hell has no use for you, and heaven doesn't want you."

Patricia screamed at him. "I'm a good person!"

"You're dead," Eddie exploded. "And I will kill you again."

Why is it that I attract some of the most diabolical criminal minds? It is one more way for the devil to come knocking at my door, I suppose. They come to me to find a way out of the concrete cell, looking to reconnect with the world outside of prison walls. They speak to me as though they know me, feel me. Some even bring me down the road of death. The steel bars cannot isolate or constrict them. The killers are not forgotten after the passage of years because they find me. They come back, through that dark escape tunnel to the open swirling portal of "the medium."

Others have done this—contacted me—but not like this. This was unfinished business. As I sat at my desk and stared at the handprint traced on his letter, I knew I had to take his hand. I had to save myself before I was taken over completely. It didn't matter anymore whether I was asleep or awake—my visions and nightmares of Patricia were constant and becoming increasingly unbearable. And facing Patricia also meant facing her murderer. I knew that now. Oh, how delighted he must be to have found me. In what lifetime does a killer get to sit and speak to his victim? Get to live again the thrill of the hunt, the rapture of the homicide? Get to control and conquer again a life he has already taken? In *my* lifetime, it turns out.

I pushed everything off my desk and smoothed out his letter. I flexed my hand and then carefully placed my fingers over his outline exactly. Our hands together were almost a perfect match. I braced myself, and then—nothing. I laughed out loud—I won!—and tried to take my hand away.

The lights went out and my hand stayed put. I felt someone approaching from behind. I heard him breathing and felt his hands on my chair. He started to hum, and swiveled my chair slightly from side to side as he stood behind me.

"Jackie," he whispered in my ear. "You know who I am. Don't lie. I don't like liars or people who take things from me . . . I used to have so much fun. You know something, Jackie? Not every girl did I kill . . . I could think of one or two . . ."

He pushed me in my chair to the door that leads to my garage.

"Look straight ahead now. Look at the door," he said. I tried to get a glimpse of him out of the corner of my eye, but he took my chin in his hands and forced my face toward the door.

"Now that I got your attention, let's have fun, okay?"

I did not answer.

"Okay?" He hissed the word forcefully through his teeth.

My voice shook. "Yes . . . okay . . ."

The top half of the door opened. I saw a red light behind it, and a woman appeared a little bit away in the distance. I could see her whole figure, clad in only a G-string and torn silk stockings. Still behind me, he placed his cheek on mine. "Keep your eyes open," he ordered.

The woman danced slowly and seductively closer to the door, flaunting her bare breasts, feeling herself for his sneaky pleasure. He snickered like a schoolboy and reached toward her but then backed off, like he'd lost his nerve. He got control of himself and then gripped me again, squeezing my face.

"This is what I loved to do. By day, I longed to be inside that filth. By night, I stalked and ate their sins."

His teeth chattered as he loosened his grip.

"Did you sin, Jackie? Did God cleanse your flesh?" He rubbed my face. "I'm so hungry I could eat you. But not yet. The games have just begun, and patience is a virtue."

He came around the chair and squatted in front of me, separating my legs with his own. It was the tall man in black. He leaned in and smelled my hair. "I will make love to your decaying body and cradle your bones. Do you know what the Gemini is?"

I said nothing. I did not know if he was going to kill me or just keep going with the torture.

"Well, let me tell you. The Gemini is two. I'm missing one. The Gemini is what we are all made up of. The good and the bad. God and the devil. You and your mother."

I sat, frozen with fear, with no choice but to keep listening.

"You know, I once met a prostitute in Highland Park. Oh, my days, my glory days when I ruled the streets. That's the Gemini, that other part of me, that thing that controlled me, that gave me—a mere man—such power.

"I was looking for the right one. Something was driving me. Eddie wasn't in the driver's seat. Eddie was just the vessel.

"She came over to me. I was sitting on the top back of a bench. I could have snuffed out her life in a second. She walked her walk, putting her hand up her skirt, touching herself, telling me I could do what I wanted to her. She licked her fingers like candy.

"Do you like candy, Jackie? . . . Anyway, back to the tramp. She was something, swinging her bleached-blond hair. I sat, just watching. I didn't want what was between those legs. I wanted to take that last breath. To hold her soul. To fill my gut. I was going to rule in hell. I still will.

"I touched my fake hard-on, leading her to me. I jumped down from the bench, walking slowly around it, leading her to salvation—in my world!

"I stopped in an isolated area. She gave me a price. Little did she know how high her price was. She dropped to her knees, ready to get to work.

"My body began to twist and shake, contort into something else. I was so ready to eat, the hunger was so painful, so great. I felt my jaw crack and open wide . . . wider. My grip was powerful, my back arched like a beast. The hunt was over, my hands touched her, and I felt faint. My legs gave way."

Still in front of me, he paused in his story for just a moment and then continued.

"A dark voice inside me said, 'No, it's not her . . . That's not the one.' This never happened before. I fell backward . . . and yelled, 'Get away, you damn bitch!'"

He stopped again, and laughed. "I eventually found what I was looking for. And now she's gone, gone as though she found a crack and slid out like a slug. My slug! Jackie, do you know who I mean?"

I shook my head. My tears fell but made no difference to him.

"Well, you will hand her over. We all answer to someone. You have no use for my kill. I don't want to hurt you, but I do enjoy this."

He pushed my chair away from the door and back to my desk. "Put your hand back on that paper . . . that's right . . . back on my hand. Now you know who I am."

The room filled with the sounds of banging and knocking. I opened my eyes. My hand was still on the paper. I jerked it away, stuffed the letter back in its envelope, and hid it. I didn't want anyone to find it again. Ever.

I came up the stairs from my office out of breath and calling for Joanne. I heard a door shut and someone run from my room into hers.

"Jo, come on, I had a bad night," I called. I had hoped

she was out with her boyfriend. I didn't want her at home while I was going through all of this. I walked into my daughter's room and saw not her, but the little girl in the yellow raincoat. It was too much. I slid down to the floor and wrapped my arms around myself. I did not have the strength to stand anymore. The girl ran past me and into Joanne's closet as I sat on the floor, rocking myself and crying.

I don't know how much time passed before I roused myself. I truly couldn't take this anymore. I stomped over to the closet and started shouting for the kid. I told her I'd play with her if she came out. I grabbed everything I could reach, throwing clothes and shoes out of the closet. I stuck my hand in again and something sliced into me. I cried out in pain and yanked my hand back out, covered with blood. Shit. Joanne was going to have a fit, me getting blood all over her stuff. I ran to the bathroom and washed away most of the blood, revealing three thin slices. What the hell? I wrapped my hand in a towel and went back to the closet. More carefully now, I searched that spot again. And pulled out my razor. The one from my bathtub. The one Patricia had taken.

Did *I* put this razor blade in Joanne's closet?

My blood soaked the towel, and my fears soaked my soul. When does your reality become a nightmare? A convicted serial killer was stepping into my life. I was being stalked. I was his victim, sharing his life, becoming his sin.

ELEVEN

Will came home, happily calling, "Jackie, come give me a hug!" How I loved this man. I greeted him and tried to hide my cut hand. I was hiding so much from him now. He noticed anyway and was concerned, even though I made light of it. Then he tried to cheer me up.

"Hey, let's go out to dinner," he said.

Not tonight, I groaned to myself. I had a huge literal mess to clean up in Joanne's room, and I also didn't feel like taking the metaphorical mess that was me out into the world that night. But then I looked up to see Will's big boyish grin. It reminded me of better times, and a deep melancholy washed over me. I couldn't make his world miserable, too.

"All right," I said. "But I get to pick the place."

He laughed and told me to hurry and get ready. I went into our bedroom, and instead of changing clothes, I searched the corners and the closet and under the bed.

I found nothing and sat down, whispering, "Where are you?"

There was no answer, and so I got up and moved to the mirror to freshen up. I saw only myself in the reflection, which was a relief. "Okay, if you're in here, please don't come out now." I was whispering again, and I couldn't believe I had been reduced to begging a ghost of a woman—or worse, my nightmare man-in-black stalker—to leave me alone.

I put my lipstick on, my favorite plum color that goes so well with my black hair and light blue eyes. Still nothing from my intruders. Maybe they had both taken off! I shook my head and told myself, no more. No thoughts of them; let them sleep.

I grabbed my purse and returned to Will, who turned on his courtly charm.

"You sure look beautiful, Miss Jackie," he said in his smooth Southern accent, just like he'd sounded when we first met in New Orleans all those years ago.

"You sly old dog, Mr. Will. You sure know how to treat a lady," I said, letting my own natural drawl come out. You can take the girl and boy out of the South, but you can't take the South out of them. And since I was thinking South, how about South of the border? There was a great Mexican restaurant nearby that made the best guacamole, right at your table.

Will agreed, and I texted Joanne. *Will and I are going out to dinner. I'm sorry about your room. I was looking for something. I'll clean it up when I get in. Love you bunches. Mom.* Will pointed out, and I knew, that Joanne was an adult out doing her own thing. But I was still her mother. And we always made a point of saying we loved each other. In my line of work, I hear too many people say "if only" they had said something or another. Plus, I owed her the apology.

We walked the seven blocks to the restaurant, talking easily. How I had missed the simple joy of being next to Will and feeling safe. I saw him look at my injured hand but ignore it—we were both sort of embarrassed by it, like when the wind blows up a girl's skirt in public for a moment and everyone politely averts their gazes.

I quickly changed the topic, and our conversation once again became easy. It was all so real—the cool breeze blowing my hair, the leaves on the ground, autumn upon us. I had no idea where the time had gone, and I meant more than just the seasons.

I remembered when I could reach my hand out and grab life. It wasn't that long ago when it was a race that I was winning. When it felt good to breathe heavily and feel the adrenaline kick in. I could look behind me for my opponents, because I was outrunning everything. Feeling the victory. And then I turned a corner and ran smack into one of them. I never thought it would get ahead of me and lie in wait. The whole time I was looking over my shoulder, it was one step ahead, waiting for me.

I grabbed on to Will's arm, pulling him closer and trying to shake off my gloom. The twinkling lights of the restaurant appeared out of the dusk. It was done up in a Day of the Dead theme. How appropriate.

We walked in and I stopped, just to take it in. Most

people came for the margaritas and the cursory feel of a different culture. They didn't know what I did. For instance, the altar with its many offerings, which was placed in the back in order to protect the entire restaurant. Evil would see this Madonna and hightail it out. On my way past the cash register to our table, I saw a protection bag and red candle next to it. These proprietors were fully aware of what lurked beneath the surface.

Next to the cash register sat an old woman, probably the owner's grandmother. Her gray hair was pulled back neatly from a face lined with wrinkles and wisdom. Her gaze followed me, and she started speaking in Spanish. She began to rock slowly as though pushing forward the Holy Ghost. She picked up momentum and made the sign of the cross. That old lady knew.

I sat down at our table with her eyes burning into my back, her chants calling her God. Warning him of an intruder.

I sat across the table from Will and looked around at the fantastical masks on the walls of the restaurant. Will was talking, but I stopped paying attention to him when I saw the mouth slits on the masks move, as though they were talking, too. I shifted uneasily in my seat. A waiter stirred a large barrel of homemade sangria. The fruity scent turned metallic in my nostrils, and it looked thick as blood when he raised his big wooden spoon, the drops splashing loudly back into the barrel.

I turned away and focused on that altar in the back. The eyes of the Madonna came to life and stared right at me. I called out silently to her for mercy and strength.

Suddenly, I felt nauseated. I asked Will to order for me as I hauled myself to my feet. He looked concerned as he grabbed my hand. I couldn't let him know. I made a crack about having to use the ladies' room and pulled away. I gave him a shaky smile and walked toward the back, past the altar with its lit candles. The flames rose higher and then began to go out as I walked past.

I felt light-headed as I went down the narrow stairs to the bathrooms. There was a sharp pain in my stomach, as though something was scratching its way out. I could feel it coming. *Please, not here*, I thought.

I pushed open the bathroom door, threw my purse on the counter, and gripped it tightly. My head down, I began to rock with the hope that I could push out the entity, the poison, the chaos, the delusions. I started to pray.

I grabbed a paper cloth off the stack and swiped at the sweat on my forehead. Then the lights dimmed and all of the hand dryers went on one at a time. Water started to seep from the grout between the floor tiles as I heard a woman in one of the stalls. Steam blasted from the old radiator as I slid my feet on the wet floor toward the row of stalls and checked them one by one. All were empty except the last one. That old, familiar voice called to me as I stood directly in front of the door. I backed up against the wall directly opposite as her face appeared in the crack between the stalls. I could see her long, straggly hair and wild eyes.

"Can't a lady take a pee?" Patricia cackled. "That was some good line you used on old Mr. Will. Hey! Pass me some toilet paper. And don't try to wish me away! I think Will likes me better."

The door swung open, and she stood before me, her body reeking of old death and her shirt covered in knife holes.

"Did you think you could hide me, and I don't deserve to go out?"

I stood still, pressed against the wall as she came closer, demanding that I look at her. Her features were long gone, decayed away. Her mouth opened, exposing a dark hole.

"Come closer to me. Kiss me, Jackie." Her hot breath caressed my lips. I looked directly into her eyes and saw her fear, saw her begging for help. Cries from the beyond spilled out of me.

And then I was fine. Finally. I opened my eyes and was back in front of the big bathroom mirror. I looked my fine self over for a minute. Just like a lady, I took the paper cloth I found in my hand and wiped off my lipstick. It was so not my color. And my shirt—I looked like a prude. I undid the top two buttons of my blouse, reached into my bra, and pulled out a tube of pink lipstick I'd hidden there. Pucker up, baby. Around and around my lips it went. *Now* I looked good!

I started to shove the lipstick back in my bra, but stopped. I couldn't take my eyes off my reflection, with my bright lips and smeared mascara. So beautiful. I reached toward the mirror and with my lipstick wrote in big, bold, sticky pink letters. *PATRICIA.*

I stood back and admired everything. *Mirror, mirror, on the wall, who's the one wanted by all . . .*

The door swung open, and two old women interrupted me. I glared at them, but they didn't notice me. I hated it when people didn't see me, and it happened all the time. They were dressed differently—longer dresses, small hats, shiny heels. Old-fashioned and way too proper for me. I slid to the side so I could listen. I felt a little embarrassed and noticed in the mirror that I was biting my fingernails.

"What a shame. That poor child missing now for over a month. You know, that's all they found. Her little yellow raincoat. I hear it was covered in blood."

"No! She was only eight years old. What a shame."

I felt a pull inside me, like someone was responding to their words and trying to get out. I pushed her back and looked at myself again in the mirror. This time, I didn't look pretty. A white, wiggling maggot was slithering out of the corner of my mouth. I pulled it out and threw it away from me, feeling gross and disgusting. I bent over the sink and swished water around my mouth, trying to spit out the remainders of death. The two women ignored me. They turned and walked right through the bathroom door, fading away. I ran after them . . .

. . . **What had happened?** I was standing upstairs, on the restaurant's main floor, surrounded by the ordinary sounds of happy conversations and clinking utensils. How much time had gone by? I looked at my cell phone, trying to figure it out.

I finally saw our table and Will as he sat facing away from me. As I walked toward him, people started shooting odd looks my way and whispering to one another. I kept going and rubbed my husband's back as I passed by him and took my place at our table.

"Hey, you. Why didn't you check up on me?" I said, my head down as I placed my napkin neatly in my lap. Then I looked over at him and smiled. He spit out his drink in shock and stared at me, mouth agape. I stared back. What the hell was his problem? I followed his gaze down and noticed that my blouse had several buttons unfastened. I was flaunting much more cleavage than I ever did. I reached up and felt my face. My hands came away covered with sticky pink lipstick and smeared black mascara.

I started to bristle at the look on his face. He took notice, and his expression switched to one of worry. He reached for my hand.

"Let me in, Jackie. I love you."

"You wouldn't understand. I don't even understand," I said. "I'm not going to a doctor. There isn't a prescription for this. Maybe a mental institution . . ." I laughed, though it was the furthest thing from funny.

I looked into his eyes and saw all the obstacles we had overcome, all the dangers we had conquered—together. Both of us knew things that most people did not even realize existed.

"Will, did you ever get a splinter, not knowing how or when it happened? But you can see something under your skin—the shape of it making the outer part of the flesh inflamed, raised up. And you begin to pick at it with a sharp pair of tweezers, pulling back the skin to expose this object that's infecting your finger. And you grab it, trying to slide it out. You'll do anything to relieve the throbbing. Well, that is what I'm going through. But it's not a splinter."

Will slowly leaned back in his chair. "What happened when you went to the bathroom? You come back looking different. Your makeup is running down your face; your lipstick is a color you don't wear and never liked."

I could feel my occupant becoming furious. Will was criticizing her directly. Her rage built. I tried to keep her down, but it was so hard. She was so powerful.

I told Will I would wait outside while he paid the bill. He protested—he had asked for the dessert tray. Ah, my man. He knew that if anything would get me to stay, it was my sweet tooth.

The waiter approached and placed the platter of Mexican delights in front of me. He leaned in toward my ear and started to tell me which one was best. In seconds, though, his smooth sales pitch became a deep, hollow snarl.

"Keep looking straight ahead into that window of the kitchen door. Do you see who you are now?"

I saw men in white medical-examiner uniforms lifting a woman. Her face passed the glass window in the door, disfigured from the murder and exposure to the elements afterward. The men brought her directly by me, commenting on the countless stab wounds that had to be the work of that serial killer on the loose. Just behind them, I saw myself walking slowly and mechanically in the same direction. The image was solid, and I watched as the vision of me passed by. I was carrying a child in my arms—the little girl in the yellow raincoat.

The restaurant's kitchen door swung open and the red ball I had seen the little girl carrying came bouncing straight toward me. I jumped away from the table, knocking things over, trying to get away. Will grabbed my arm, threw down enough money to cover the dinner and my antics, and dragged my sobbing self out to the sidewalk. He wrapped his arms around me.

"Jackie, you're not alone. You never were. And I'm not going to let anything or anyone hurt you. I made that promise a lifetime ago."

We started to walk, and I started to talk. I told him of the horrible things I was seeing, of trying to mimic ordinary people and their actions because I was unable to act normally.

"I'm being pulled from both sides. There is this guy who just appears out of nowhere, dressed in black and holding me hostage," I said. "And then there's this woman, who makes me do things I don't want to, and this little girl who I've seen my whole life. She's somehow in the thick of it. The guy wants the woman. And the child and the woman both keep running."

Will listened carefully—like he always did—and waited

for me to continue. When I didn't, he decided to push the subject further himself.

"Jackie," he said slowly, "I found a large storage box tied up and hidden in the back of the garage. How do you know the New York City Zodiac?"

I felt like I'd been busted. Deny, deny, deny.

"I don't know him. How would I know him? The woman who sometimes controls me knows him."

Will fired back. "How did he get our address? Why do you hide his letters? Drawings, his hair—"

"She gave the address to him! Maybe she wants answers, maybe she wants . . ." I stopped. "Maybe . . . she wants freedom." I heard the words come out, but it didn't sound like me. It was a sad voice that ran over mine, like two people talking at once. I stood on the sidewalk and wondered about what I had just heard put into words.

Will, still concerned and upset, stomped inside to take a shower, and I headed off to check on the Zodiac box. I ran downstairs to the garage the minute I heard the water go on. I locked the door behind me and pulled out the box. I needed to make sure nothing was gone. Or, more accurately, that nothing had escaped.

The single lightbulb hanging above me began to crackle. I looked up at it and heard a quick scrape on the concrete floor behind a large CD rack we stored down here. Then came a gurgling sound mixed with laughter. I followed it around the CD rack, and there she was. Patricia, bent into a position on my garage floor that was not humanly possible—if one were alive.

Her face was wet and gray and framed by her tangled, stringy hair. Her eye sockets looked like dark holes, and she foamed at the mouth, spitting words at me I couldn't understand. She was strapped into a straitjacket and was struggling to free herself. She tried to stand, with the inhuman strength I have only ever seen during the horrifying events of an exorcism.

I fell backward in terror and must have screamed, because I heard Joanne and then Will trying to get into the garage through the main car door. Will yelled at Joanne to get out of the way. They punched at the code panel, and the door began to rise. Will slid underneath and rushed past me. No, right through me. I looked down at myself and stretched out my arms. They couldn't see me or hear me. They disappeared behind the oversize CD tower.

I turned back toward the garage door as it finished raising up. And there he was. The tall man in black, holding a large knife. I turned and saw Will and Joanne on their knees, struggling with something. I couldn't figure out what was going on. I turned back to the man, who grinned.

"Only I can hear you," he said. "Take the knife, Jackie, and join me forever. Feel the power; let me live in you. You are my Gemini. We are all two. We are all evil. Let me wrap my arms around you."

I did not want to be here. I did not want to be part of this. I felt so alone. And then someone took my hand. I looked down and saw the little girl in the yellow raincoat looking up at me, a spirit beside me.

"He's the stranger, isn't he?" she asked, looking up at me.

I saw the strangulation marks around her neck. And I remembered.

A calendar hung on the kitchen wall. November 1950. The picture was of little puppy dogs playing in a red basket. The room was dark, lit only by the candles on a birthday cake in the middle of the table. A little girl sat in front of it, perched up on her knees, and leaned forward to blow them out. Her father told her to make a wish. Then her mother stopped her and ran to retrieve another present to add to the pile.

"I have one more surprise for you," she said, peeling back the wrapping. It was a yellow raincoat.

"Oh, Mommy, thank you so much! I love it! I love it! Can I wear it today? Please, Mommy?"

"We'll see," the mother said, smiling at her beautiful birthday girl. "Now, blow those candles out. You're a big girl now."

She leaned forward again, clutching her worn teddy bear, and blew.

The lights went out. Something leaned in very close and whispered a wish. *I'm coming back.*

The lights came on, and the kitchen had changed. The party was gone. The calendar hung crookedly on its peg. The mother and father sat huddled together at the table. The mother clutched at the raincoat and started screaming.

"Who took my daughter? I want her back. This is all I have of my baby . . . Someone took our baby girl."

The girl stood next to me as we watched the scene. The raincoat she wore was dripping with rain. The drops became blood and pooled around my feet. I couldn't move. She took my hand.

"I was killed by a man," she said. I looked into her eyes and she showed me.

Now, as I heard Will and Joanne struggling behind me, I knew they couldn't see or hear me. I knew how the dead felt. I knew why they so readily came to me. They just wanted someone to listen. And dear God, right now, so did I. I was just like that little girl next to me. I might *be* that girl next to me. I held her hand, that little girl who couldn't run, who couldn't get away. Just like Patricia, and just like me.

And she had run to the only person who could see her. I closed my eyes to shut out the Zodiac standing in my garage and took a breath. The air came out in a rush as my eyes flew open, and I saw Will and Joanne standing over me. I was lying on the floor of my garage—behind the CD tower—kicking and screaming.

"It's okay. It's only us," Will said, holding his hands up so I could see them. "Look, I have nothing. It's me."

Joanne sank down on the floor next to me, her eyes wide. I stopped screaming and started crying. Will asked if I'd fallen and gotten hurt. I shook my head no and managed to ask, "What happened?"

They both had heard bloodcurdling screams coming from the garage. It didn't sound like me, and they thought someone had broken into the house. They had found me in the corner in a trans-medium state—I was rocking back and forth and talking in two different voices, a woman and a man who seemed to be arguing.

As I calmed down, Will turned to the large sketch pad that lay next to me. On it, I had scrawled in red crayon:

My name used to be Jane. I'm eight years old, and I was murdered, too.

Will carefully picked up the pad. Underneath it was one of my large kitchen knives. The knife was all scratched, and the concrete floor around me had deep gouges in it. Will snatched it quickly and moved it away from me. I hung my head.

"I'm going to get put away again," I said weakly.

Both my husband and my daughter stared at me, uncomprehending.

"What! Jackie, why would you say that?" Will said. He knew that I had never been "put away" for anything in my entire life.

My voice was barely audible. "I don't know . . . because *she* was . . ."

Will—still carefully holding the knife away from me—told Joanne to take me upstairs to bed while he cleaned up the mess.

"No!" I leaped to my feet. "I want everything back, now!" I grabbed everything and packed it away in the box. "I'm telling you both, stay away from my things, or he'll kill you."

As I packed everything away and tried to catch my breath, a startling realization took hold of me. The tall man in black was the twin of the Zodiac. He was the devil behind Eddie's meek smile. It wasn't enough to murder; he had to keep their souls. He had to keep his victims from finding the arms of God. It was a double win. He victimized them for all eternity and delivered a slap to the face of the Almighty. Is there a war between heaven and hell? You bet there is.

And Eddie was an exceptional soldier. The devil took the features of his DNA—his mirrored image—and left that concrete cell to finish his work. Eddie's physical body could not leave, but that powerful devil inside him was free. He could walk along undetected in order to collect more trophies, and reclaim the one who got away.

TWELVE

―――――◆―――――

At one time or another, we all have something in common—we all get stuck. We all get in our own way. Advanced degrees and overflowing bank accounts can't help. Sometimes, the more we have, the more cynical we become. We may find ourselves acting differently, becoming distant and distracted. It can happen at any age, to any one of us. It can disguise itself as unhappiness, emptiness. Often we see it but blame others. We can begin to destroy important relationships in the quest to find the answer to that single word—*why?*

Some of us have no choice but to answer this question. The glass of water that represents your soul starts to evaporate. Every morning, you crawl out of bed to examine the glass and you notice that there is less and less water. You see the stale lines where the old water was, and as you stare at those high-water marks every day, the lines become more prominent than the water itself. All you can see is the depletion of your inner happiness, your core, your soul.

By the time people like this seek me out, they have lost their bearings. They often do not even know what their real problem is, just that they no longer feel right. My hope for these people is always the same—that they find me before they destroy their current lives, their families, their relationships. So many of them say the same thing: "Jackie, I don't know who I am anymore. My thoughts and wants are scattered." So I sit them down, and we begin. The key to contentment is finding the door you never knew existed. You may have to go back to move forward. You will need to enhance your senses and truly see for the first time. In doing so, chances are you'll shed years of sorrow that you never even knew you carried.

I begin by making my clients comfortable, just chatting. They're often unaware that what I am looking for is the children they once were—not in this present lifetime but in their past lives. People tend to get stuck at the age that significant past events took place. For example, if someone died in childbirth in a former life, that person will now likely fear the idea of becoming a mother and associate it with heartbreak, yet long for it at the same time. Or take a man who suddenly begins to avoid his family and job. He blames everything he can think of for this behavior, because he does not know the truth—that he died at that exact age in a previous life, and he has no idea what to do with the rest of his current one.

And so I take them back to the time when they were

most happy and carefree, typically between the ages of eight and twelve, when they were still innocent. I always set my exercises in a lovely place, abundant with natural beauty. Wildflowers are waist high and sway slowly in the breeze. A magical road runs through it all, and on the other side stands a mystical forest with trees of every shape and size. The sun bounces off every leaf. Tiny animals scurry around to greet them, peeking out from the under-brush to see this child they once were.

The child begins to get shaded in, like a figure being colored with a crayon. First the hair, the face, the eyes . . . Everything is described, including what the child is wear-ing. And every time I do this exercise, there is a unique choice of clothing that immediately tells me what era we're in. Is the child wearing buttons or zippers or Velcro? Holding a wooden toy or a plastic one?

After we re-create this lost soul they now recognize, I stand before them and take their hands. They are not alone. We walk along the road. To the right is a fabulous garden, drenched in color like a Monet painting. To the left is a fairy-tale land, with tiny people who keep the for-est safe, bushes that grow cream puffs, and clouds of mouthwatering cream. Everything makes sense to the child's eyes.

We walk along this road until we reach the top of a hill and see their childhood home in the distance. As we get closer, the dwelling becomes clearer and they describe it to me. There is no pain or hurt, even if it represents hor-ror. All of that has been washed away by this marvelous land. They point and show me the window to their bedroom, the front door, the mailbox that stands just down the road.

The door opens and out comes the adult version of themselves, who has waited anxiously for years to be reunited. They run to each other, and tears run like a river, but in this case, the river runs both ways. I stand back and watch the reunion of a soul. The adult hugs the child, and they grasp each other's hands. This is their safe place now. They talk and walk. They'll remember this healing conversation, and they'll never forget or leave themselves behind again. They'll fix the current wrong and dry the old tears away.

We cannot fix the future without confronting the past. It's never easy, but it is—ultimately—for the best. I have taken thousands down this road throughout my career as a spiritual medium and counselor for the soul. I have uncovered and documented many past lives, helping others to understand.

And now, it was my turn. I knew the picture, because I painted it. And I knew that I needed to go further inside it. But it was so dangerous to do to myself. I knew that I could get stuck in between my current life and my previous one, trapped forever in a no-man's land, if I relived my previous death. I had done this for other people, but that was different. There was always enough distance between my own life and what I was experiencing for them that I stayed safe. But this *was* my own life. And my own death. I could die from the fear of it. But not knowing my own past could kill my future. I kept seeing this Jane in a yellow raincoat. She was trying to tell me something. What was it?

* * *

I remembered waking up in my own childhood bed, on my own eighth birthday, screaming that I had been killed. My parents rushed in, and my dad, the great medicine man, started chanting for my wolf spirit guide to come and protect me. My mom just wiped my face with a cold, wet cloth. Then she pulled back the covers, and I saw the shock on her face. She quickly started to wash my feet, which were covered in blood.

My parents never asked how I got blood on me. They already knew what I was capable of—that leaving this world and interacting with the dead was as natural for me as going outside to play. But this incident I pushed as far away as I possibly could, deep into my mind. I convinced myself that it was not my memory. We all remember things we never did or saw, things from a previous life. The only difference was that my slate had not wiped clean when I returned for this life. Did the same blood my mother washed away that day still run through me?

Eddie began to call me from prison on a regular basis. Sometimes I would take notes, and sometimes I would record our conversations. When I did that, though, I always told him I was doing it (which I do whenever I record someone, no matter who it is), and he would suddenly get shy and start mumbling his words. His real torrents of talk came when posterity wasn't listening.

He would mutter and he would ramble, and sometimes,

he would even answer my questions. One day, I asked him if he knew why his victim had come back. He became very quiet, but the silence over the phone line was thick, like a heavy snow falling. After a moment, a very sure voice that did not sound like him started to speak.

"Because she wants to live again. She wants to be with you. She wants your skin. But now we have a big problem, Jackie. This leaves me in the middle of you both. I'm down a soul . . . I hope you understand my situation. You have this ongoing fight to save the souls—dead or alive . . . We are all soldiers, just on different sides." He paused slightly. "I don't like her picking up the phone when I call you. I don't speak to my kill. I hunt. I haunt."

He turned his attention from Patricia to me. "I live in your dreams now. I walk with you; I eat with you; I snuggle in bed with you. Because I can. I can tell you this, Jackie. If Patricia possesses you, it's done—lights out."

If that possession (which I had been fighting against for months) did succeed, then one of two things could happen, he said. I would die again in that park on a steamy summer night. Or—and this was the big, directly-on-target fear of mine, and that bastard knew it—I would end up in an asylum. I had always worried about that, considering that some people think it's crazy to talk to the dead. But if I *became* the dead? If I was fully possessed? I'd get locked away for sure, and that terrified me.

"I can see the flashing lights as the juice gets turned up on that electrical shock therapy machine," he taunted. "Don't think they still don't zap. Then you get to shuffle around all medicated up. Not a pretty picture . . . Just

My daughter, Joanne Agnelli, and me. *(Will Barrett)*

My husband, Will Barrett, and me. *(Joanne Agnelli)*

Unless otherwise noted, all photos are from author Jackie Barrett.

New York's old Bellevue Psychiatric Hospital, which now serves as a homeless men's shelter. *(Joanne Agnelli)*

The old Bellevue psychiatric ward was once home to countless souls tortured by mental illness. It is located a few blocks away from the current Bellevue Hospital Center, which is New York City's premier public hospital. *(Joanne Agnelli)*

A photo of Heriberto "Eddie" Seda taken while he was in prison.

One of the first letters I remember getting from Eddie. My hand fit perfectly in his handprint.

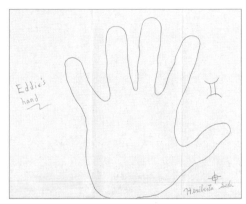

A letter Eddie sent me illustrating how he thinks the stars connect the two of us.

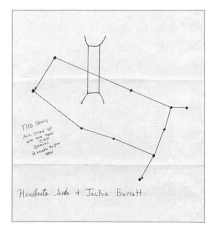

Eddie sent me the mask he wore during the rituals he would conduct before roaming the New York streets searching for people to kill.

Eddie included this letter with the mask.

When I tried on Eddie's mask, my right eye began bleeding from the tear duct.
(Will Barrett)

Eddie frequently urged me to look through his eyes, to become his other half. One can't truly know unless one sees through another's eyes.

Hi Jackie   25 Dec 2010

wear the mask feel me

Be me   YOU'LL HAVE MORE CODES

come 2 me

Stop fighting the power

you wont win this time

TIME is on MY SIDE

YES it is

TIME is on MY SIDE it is

YES it is

I see you all the time - time

Give her back & your free
Jackie you'll never win   I wont her Back!   EDDIE ♥ ☺

In the same package as the mask, Eddie also sent the bandana that he'd worn out on the streets.

Will and me with the box where I stored all of Eddie's letters, the mask, and the bandana. *(Joanne Agnelli)*

Another photo Eddie sent me of himself. He does not appear to have aged at all in the more than fifteen years he has been in prison.

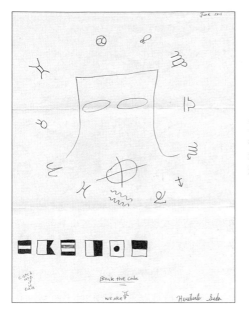

Eddie loves codes and sends me different ones, asking if I can solve them.

Eddie's bloodlust has not dimmed at all since his days stalking New Yorkers. Now, however, his focus is on me.

LOOK AT ME AS YOUR Santa ClAuS And it's YOUR BLACK ChRiSTMAS & YOU HAVE BEEN VERY NAUGHTY

WHO AM I ?

Hi Jackie   30 July 2010

Finally ! yes we must all wait our turn
I have forever . look at us as a Door you on one
side me on the other, you push and I pull ! HAHA

You broke the code ! IM Proud of you Jackie
but can you Catch me . Should we set a
Clock ? Will you be the little hand or BiG ?

will You finD My twin OR will He find a
New home to kill and Rush Back to Me . fill
My BELLY .

Will it Be You ? close your hands
around the Knife .

You will feel many things — you will DIE
AND BECOME — You will Be MORE . You
Will Be the GemiNi I
You will Feel ME BREATH ME
I walk with YOU, I sleep Next to you
I smell YOUR sweet flesh

You will BECOME MY kill — 100+ times you
Will Bleed — OR You CAN give HER BACK —

WHO will I BE ? the man sitting next to you on
the train ? THE Bus DRivers , tHE BAKER THE BUtcHER
THE underTAKER   Eddie

A reflection of the drawing my friend Maria DiNaso was given in a gas station bathroom during our drive to Great Meadow Correctional Facility in upstate New York. *(Will Barrett)*

A close-up of the drawing.

think, I can visit you every day, and no one will believe you. Sure, you'll run around telling anyone that will listen. That's when the real fun begins. Zap, zap, zap." His words shot through my head like bolts of pain. "I was thinking, if she can come back and live in you, take over your mind and body—well, so can I. So can I."

But he knew that I would continue to fight. And that pissed him off.

"Pure evil will always know you, Jackie, because you not only know it exists, but you keep trying to save yourself. They know you can see them. You're a fucking roadblock. You're not a priest. Most of them fear the devil, but are not trained. Give me a break! They devote their life to God and can't stand up to his brother!"

He kept at it, his voice the same steady, certain tone.

"I told you what I never told anyone, not even those priests that came to see me. Something powerful ran through my blood, gave me knowledge, showed me how to become the most feared. I felt the transformation. I knew just what spells to perform. I had the book."

I knew what he was talking about. It was the *Solomon Book of Spells*, an ancient volume of the black arts that he had used. One of the spells he cast was a blinding spell, which let him walk throughout the city without anyone seeing his real face. He could walk into a room and not be noticed. *That would explain why the descriptions his victims gave the police were of a black man*, I thought.

"The door opened and I became the NYC real nightmare. I did my job so well . . . You have the truth. So many of us 'most evil' have found that book. I don't even know where it came from. Everything was falling into place. I was given a name—the Zodiac. Runs chills through you. Yeah, it does. Copycat, my ass. Why not—recycling a name? He was never caught, no face to the work. So why not show up in New York City? We are everywhere."

"Where's that book, Eddie?" I asked.

"Oh, Jackie, it disappears for the next in line."

"Eddie, I think you hid it right before you got caught. That was the plan the devil had. To use you. Then hide the book of spells, let someone else find it and pick up where you left off," I said. "But, Eddie, if I find it first . . ."

"He will never let you find that! You dare test the devil at his own game? You'll wind up just like your mother."

The devil made sure he accomplished many of his deeds, Eddie said. But then, I asked, why did he want Patricia back? He already killed her. Wasn't that enough?

"You interfered! Giving shelter to the dead, showing them the way home." His voice rose in anger. "Now he brought me back. You are not authorized to fight me! How dare you, Jackie, go against God. God lets the devil have his way, so people are forced to believe in him! Get on your knees, Jackie."

He was yelling now. I knew he was pushing my every button, trying to get me to come to his side. Finding the weak cracks is the sly work of Lucifer. I bowed my head, even though he couldn't see me, and a prayer went through my brain. *For I am weak, Lord. Stand by me, the power and the goodness. I ask only for strength.*

Eddie went quiet, as though I had spoken the words, which I had not. "Are you done, Jackie?"

I was not done, not by a long shot, and someday, he would know it.

I repeated that prayer all the time now. Patricia, although not a demon, was definitely making my life a living hell. As we entered our second year together, I would forget birthdays and anniversaries. I couldn't remember how to use modern electronics that hadn't been around when she was alive—my big television remote, my computer. I maxed out credit cards and kept not paying the mortgage. I shut off the power because Patricia thought it would be fun to just use candles. I went to my safe-deposit box at the bank, and next to the expensive jewelry I had collected during my world travels, I found plastic rings out of a toy vending machine and other silly trinkets. So much for that being a secure place to put things.

I did things I would never, ever do—that went against everything I believed. I jumped turnstiles. I shoplifted. I drank alcohol. I went to dangerous neighborhoods and hung out with dangerous people. Joanne was so worried about my erratic behavior that she put all of my medical records and my name and address in my cell phone, so if something happened to me, it would be easier for the authorities to figure out who I was. Sometimes I had to pull up the address myself to find my way home.

I began to think about ending my torment. I could take us both home and say "Fuck you" to the devil at the same time. I could kill myself, and he would no longer be able to try to enlist me into his army. But I knew where suicide victims went. It is not the hell ruled by the devil but a hell of their own construction—a hell of sorrow, of confusion, of not forgiving oneself. It is a waiting room of loneliness. It is populated not by bad people but by unhappy souls waiting to be rescued by their loved ones. I had visited this place many times, releasing souls, at the request of their loved ones, and showing them a way out. And often, I'm able to answer that lingering question for those left alive. Why?

I knew I should not take that path. But it was starting to look very, very tempting.

I awoke to the sound of rain hitting hard against my bedroom windows. The chimes on the patio clattered in the wind, picking up the rhythm of the fall chill. I listened to the sounds, knowing I had to go out. Next to me, Will was sound asleep and unaware. It was fairly early in the evening—probably 10:00 p.m.—but totally dark. I turned on no lights as I dressed. I laced up my black boots, feeling an inexplicable surrender as I did so, and threw on my black jacket—not a raincoat, a purposeful choice because I had started to like the damp feeling of the rain soaking down deep into my bones. I felt the wetness but was numb to the cold.

I came into the dark living room, sat in an armchair with my hat in my hands, and waited for my instructions. They would come from a man who sat in solitary confinement. It had taken me a long time to realize that the dark spirit that grew and lived within him was able to lift up and travel beyond the prison walls. It could move from person to person and take on his features and character- istics without the host ever knowing that a hitchhiker was aboard. Or to me, at least, he could come alone.

I sat and listened to the late night traffic, tires splashing through the puddles in the street outside. And then still- ness took its place, followed by a low hum in my ears. The wood floor creaked beneath me, and the air moved behind me. I knew he was there, like a blind person with a cane knows there is something in his path before he reaches it. Tap, tap, tap. There it is.

I turned around slowly, squeezing my hat as though it was my only security. The dark shadow stood in the corner against the kitchen counter. The form began to solidify as it reached across the counter and took the lid off my candy dish, fully stocked because it was almost Halloween. The tall man in black scooped up a handful of candy corn.

"You know how to treat a guest," he said. "Getting my favorite candy—you know, Jackie, I have a sweet tooth. Not many can satisfy it."

He smirked at me and rolled the candy corn around in his mouth as he stared at me with his dark eyes. It felt like he was seeing deep into my soul and taking a twisted pleasure in it.

My iPod, which stood in its speaker-charger on the counter behind him, started to play. It flipped through songs like an old radio tuner—static in between different bits of music and talking. It stopped on a news bulle- tin . . . *the New York Zodiac strikes again* . . . and then switched to a sixties music station . . . *When I look out my window, many sights to see. And when I look in my window, so many different people to be . . .*

He began to dance seductively and motioned me over. I stood up and went closer, until I was only a foot away from him. . . *That it's strange, so strange, you've got to pick up every stitch . . . Must be the season of the witch . . .* As he danced, he pulled a combat knife out from under his black jacket—the same jacket I wore. He slid it over his body as though he were making love to it and then grabbed me and pulled me toward him. His face reflected in the blade before he ran it over my cheeks.

"How does it feel?" he whispered. "How does it feel, Jackie, to wear my shoes? To watch me? To follow my moves?" He looked down at my boots and back up at my face. "What shall I do with you, Jackie?"

He grabbed the back of my head and moved it closer to his. "Take this," he said as he forced a candy corn from his mouth to mine. I tried to turn my face away but couldn't. Our bodies were pressed together as one. I could feel the candy moving around in my mouth, wiggling around as if it had tentacles. His arms wrapped around me and pain pierced my middle. All I could think was that he had stabbed me and I was going to die in my own kitchen. And no one would know the truth.

He let go of me and tossed more candy into his mouth. I looked down and touched my stomach. My hand came away covered in blood. And then the phone rang. I ran for it, expecting him to stop me, but all he did was slide over next to me as I looked at the caller ID.

Great Meadow Correctional Facility.

Two places at once. I pressed 3 to accept the call.

The Eddie standing next to me chortled. "Speak up. I love eavesdropping."

I spoke into the phone. "Eddie, you're standing right next to me!"

The Eddie in prison answered back. "I called to tell you, your job is to let the world know it lives. It gets stronger and moves faster with denial."

The "it" Eddie in prison was referring to, the devil man in black standing next to me, mocked his twin. "Blah, blah, blah—he's such a baby. Acting like a bitch. It was him who created me. Him who has committed the mortal sins, the one that slapped God."

He pulled the phone out of my hand and hung it up, then grabbed my face and squeezed.

"Jackie, how does it feel to lose your mind? To be the victim? To be schizophrenic? Homeless?"

He squeezed harder, then ordered me to look at my stomach. The stab wound and the blood were gone.

"Don't think I'm done with you yet. I owe you ninety-nine more," he snarled. "How does it feel to die while you look in my eyes? How does it feel when you prowl the dark, dank streets like the beast that grows inside of you? It is you who confronted me, Jackie. You mock the devil and defy Jesus by having such a gift."

He pushed me away from him, and I hit the kitchen counter. I stood for a moment, breathing heavily. The knife was in my hand now. My fingers tightened around its handle as the blade spoke to me. *Turn around and get him now!* I held the knife high above me, spun around and leaped forward for the kill. My first kill. I was dressed head to toe in black. My boots fit perfectly.

But it wasn't the man in black. Instead, Will yelled out in surprise and grabbed my arm. He shook the knife out of my hand, and it clattered to the floor. I was no match for someone his size, thank God. I looked into his eyes, full of hurt and questions, and threw myself into his arms as I burst into sobs.

He cradled me as he kicked the knife away from us. I told him I was becoming something sinister. Me and the man in black. "He was in our kitchen, dancing, eating candy. He stabbed me, but it's gone. Look!"

I showed Will my smooth, unwounded stomach. The poor man stared at me.

"Jackie, I saw you leaning up against the kitchen counter, talking in two voices—a man and yours—and that song blasting. 'Season of the Witch.' You holding that knife. Where did you get such a knife?"

He was here, I swore. He was here. And he was there, at the prison. He could be anywhere. Or anyone.

Eddie wrote me regularly from prison. Simple notebook paper, like schoolchildren use. Covered with horror and bloodlust.

Hi Jackie

Finally! Yes we must all wait our turn
I have forever. Look at us as a door you on one

Side me on the other, you push and I pull! Ha ha
You broke the code! I'm proud of you Jackie
But can you catch me. Should we set a
clock? Will you be the little hand or big?
Will you find my twin or will he find a
new home to kill and rush back to me. fill
my belly.
Will it be you? Close your hands
around the knife.
You will feel many things—you will die
And become—you will be more. You
Will be the Gemini. [sign]
You will feel me breath [sic] me
I walk with you. I sleep next to you
I smell your sweet flesh
You will become my kill—100+ times you
Will bleed—or you can give her back—
Who will I be? The man sitting next to you on
The train? The bus drivers
the baker
the butcher
the undertaker

As usual, he signed it "Eddie" and included the Gemini symbol. He had been writing to me for several months now, and he would often include words in the margins. In this letter, he'd included a holiday send-off, even though it was only July: "*look at [sign] me as your Santa Claus and its your black Christmas and you have been very naughty*"

THIRTEEN

———————

I woke up in the middle of the night, like I'd been doing for months. Everything was quiet and still. I slipped out of bed and went over to my bedroom window. The stars outside seemed brighter and more prominent than usual. I put my finger on the glass and traced the paths between the stars. The glass was cold as my fingertips squeaked along, connecting the dots.

I heard rustling and turned to peek through the cracks in the dressing screen that hid the window from the rest of the room. Will tossed and turned in bed. I looked back at the glass and saw what I had drawn. The sign of the Gemini. The stars beyond my window blinked out, and the sky turned completely black, as if a raven—the sign of death—was covering everything with its outstretched wings. I closed my eyes and grabbed the window frame for a moment, then slowly crept back into bed. While others slept, he came forth, in many different forms. Would I have to see them all?

The doorbell rang. It was the mailman, my regular guy. "Morning, Jackie. You got a large package from a prison. You'll need to sign." I stood there with the door only half open and avoided his gaze. "Are you okay?" he asked. "You look a little thin, a little pale." I wanted nothing more than to shut the door in his face.

"Go away," I whispered. He did not hear me.

He chatted for a minute about his latest home-improvement project and then finally managed to make eye contact. "Jackie, take the pen."

My hand began to shake as I stared at this plain cardboard box. I scribbled my signature and then paused, making sure that I had signed my name, and not someone else's. Patricia was not asserting herself, but I still had the feeling that this was going to be a very bad day. I took the box from my oblivious mailman and carried it inside like I was holding a bomb. I set the alarm, went downstairs, and locked myself in my office. I sat with it on the floor. My heart began to pound and my palms to sweat.

During the months that we had been communicating, the temporal Eddie had sent me letters, artwork, clues, symbols, codes. Nothing had ever come in a box like this, however. I slowly opened it and looked inside.

On the top, there was a thick gun-parts catalog—672 pages of information on what seemed like every kind of weapon known to man. Somehow, and I still have no idea how, he had managed to get it through the prison mail screening—normally, inmates would not be allowed access to an entire book full of weapons. And he had sent it on to me to show that he could obtain anything he wanted. The rest of the package showed me that he could also hide anything he wanted, for as long as he felt like it.

Next came a full paper bag. I did not know what to expect, and there was no way in hell I was just going to stick my hand inside. Instead, I turned it upside down and shook it. And out fell two Zodiac masks.

I stared at them in horror, these lumps of material festering on my office floor. This was what his victims saw, and if they had been chosen to survive, I was quite sure it was something they would never forget. There was the bandanna, black with white designs, and a stain that had to be blood. That was what he had worn as he prowled the streets in the dark, covering his face so that only his eyes showed. He had laughed when he told me on the phone that he'd looked like the villain in an old cowboy movie.

Then there was the one no one had seen. He had worn this while hidden in his room, before he emerged to kill. This was his psych-himself-up mask. Evil oozed from every thread. It was an old black ski hat, with eyeholes and a nose slit cut into the cloth. And in red—right in the middle of the forehead—was a faded but still unmistakable sign of the Zodiac. That familiar bull's-eye symbol stared up at me, and I knew I was the next target. He was trying to groom me into becoming his other half. Patricia wasn't enough. His mission was now to make *me* a part of him. So that I would help with the massacre he was planning. The one that hadn't happened yet.

I sat on my floor with these things in front of me and noticed the paper that had fallen out with everything else. It was folded several times. I smoothed it open with dread. Eddie had scrawled phrases all over the page.

Hi Jackie

now that you broke the codes of my identity
How many am I
wear my mask. It has my hair in it
Plus the hair I sent you
we are 2 the good & bad
This is the Zodiac speaking
See through my eyes
Wear it, see me, feel me, Be me
You will never forget me
All my secrets "live in you" aways [sic]
we are both possessed
your [sic] never alone
Don't forget to look in the mirror you are me now
How many parts of the soul? As many as you can hold!
Come closer closer closer did you feel that?

He had drawn his ski mask next to the line where he said, "Wear it, see me, feel me, Be me." And he'd decorated the whole thing with several Gemini and zodiac signs.

I don't know how long I sat there staring at everything before I finally began to move.

I picked up the bandanna, and it smelled just like Eddie. It was the same smell I got from his letters and cards. That in itself wasn't unusual—we all have our own distinctive scent. But now imagine that combined with odors from a maximum-security prison. Kind of like the smell of trash mixed with the stench of an overflowing urinal. Eau de American Serial Killer.

I took up a loose floorboard and put the bandanna underneath. It seemed like it deserved its own burial place. I thought of the lives of his victims getting snuffed out, and I put the board back, nice and tight.

But every time I stepped on that spot, I sensed the remnants of the killings. The feelings of the shots burned through my body. The images of the deaths flashed through my mind. My cats hopped over the spot as though it were electrified, their body language communicating their fear. The floor creaked at night and woke me in a cold sweat. I knew I needed to find another place to hide it.

But as much as I wanted to get rid of the bandanna, I couldn't help but keep the ski mask close. I carried it with me sometimes. I even took it on the subway, just to see if people would sense something when it was nearby. Some people did—they would look down at my bag and move away. Many didn't, however, and I wondered if it was because people had become so desensitized to the evil that walked among us every day. They should really have had their guard up.

Finally, it got to be too much. I stood in front of the

mirror in my downstairs bathroom. My hands shook as I fought with myself. It was as if someone were standing next to me, slapping me, forcing this thing onto me. The mask pulled over my head. I looked in the mirror, mesmerized by the reflection of a person in the Zodiac mask. It was who I was—working in death, living in him, the victim living in me. He needed to show me firsthand, and I did see through the eyes of a monster as I stood there.

I ripped the mask off and threw it down. The sickness rushed up and out of me. I vomited all over. The pain in my stomach was like a sharp knife twisting. I curled up on the floor, trying to find a comfortable position. I felt like I was shedding old skin, molting, becoming a new thing. And all I wanted was to be an old thing—normal and ordinary and not able to see what I did.

I must have cried out, because Will banged on the door and tried to push it open, but I was in the way. Since all this started, the poor guy had had to rush in to help me so many times that it was getting ridiculous. He was big and strong, but this evil was so great, I felt I had to protect him any way I could. I felt for the mask and hid it under my body. He asked me what happened, and I lied to him, telling him I had the flu. He demanded to be let in, and I insisted that he give me a minute to wash my face. I had to hide the mask! I looked quickly around the small bathroom, and my gaze landed on the air vent in the ceiling. I stood shakily on the toilet seat and stuffed the mask inside.

Will was banging on the door again. I jerked it open, and he gaped at me.

"What happened to your eye?" he said.

How the hell should I know? I tried to brush past him. He grabbed me and brought his face close to mine. "Your eye is bleeding. Right near the tear duct."

Fantastic. I stomped up to the other bathroom and took a shower. I tried to scrub away the smell of Eddie and the sight of his murders. As I used every soap product I could get my hands on, I thought about how I could get rid of that mask without letting anyone else touch it. It was like an old genie's lamp. Rub it, and release the evil.

Will and I walked through Times Square on our way to Carmine's, a famous family-style Italian place known for its huge plates of food and good company. I hoped that a nice meal and my husband's companionship would help me shake the hold Eddie's mask had on me. As we strolled along, an overwhelming feeling of peace came over me. I wished desperately that I could hold on to it and keep it forever, but it lasted for what felt like only a split second before vanishing into the night.

We got to the crowded restaurant and were shown to our table. Will had made a reservation—that was my man, always prepared. I looked around. More than one hundred diners packed the large room, and waiters rushed here and there. As I watched, they began to move faster and faster, until they seemed to be traveling at the speed of light. The babble of voices began to fade, and the overhead lights started to sway back and forth. I had a silly thought that someone had slipped me a hallucinogenic drug and was comforted at the idea. Who would wish for that? Me, because the alternative was worse.

I excused myself and headed for the bathroom. I passed the bar and noticed one older bartender who wasn't moving as quickly as everyone else. He stood there, calmly cleaning a glass with a white cloth. He noticed me and spoke. "You can go, Jackie. William is busy and can't see you through this crowd." I stared at him and then looked back. Will was out of sight. I pushed through the door and out into the night.

Walking along Seventh Avenue, I reached into my bag and pulled out the mask. Part of me was astonished to find it. Wasn't it still stuffed in the bathroom vent? But the other part of me had known it was there, nestled close to my side, waiting to be worn.

I stopped in front of the window of an electronics shop packed with tourists. I took in my reflection, seeing Jackie but not feeling her, and pulled the mask over my head and down over my face. I gazed at the merchandise in the store, then turned to look up and around. People snapping pictures, vendors hawking purse knockoffs, billboards flashing, taxi horns blasting.

Usually, I hate these kinds of crowds more than anything. The chatter I pick up from the dead in places like this is overpowering. But that night, it didn't bother me at all. I wallowed in the chaos as I felt Eddie rushing through the crowd straight toward me. He found me on the corner, waiting for him. And in a flash, I became the biggest threat ever . . .

* * *

. . . **I turned around** slowly. My very own buffet. A piece of every continent at my fingertips. Cops were scattered about. I stood right next to three of them as they chatted together. I walked right past, laughing under my mask and saying to myself, "I did this shit before." Despite the mask pulled down over my face, no one noticed me.

There were two voices in my head. Jackie's was very quiet. I ignored it. I got to the corner of Seventh Avenue and Forty-Third Street, where they had that little NYPD building that made tourists feel safe. Ha! There were more cops here. Boy, these guys sure knew how to eat, bellies hanging over those belts loaded down with flashlights and handcuffs, mace and a gun, and now terrorist packs, too. But do you have an Eddie pack, cops? Do you?

The sweet smell of death filled the air. *This isn't real,* the quiet voice said. "Shut the fuck up, Jackie," I told it. "Listen and learn from the best. They said I had a low IQ. Yeah, fool the public so the pigs don't look so bad. I tricked these pigs for years. They didn't catch me. My master was done with me and turned me in. Now I'm back.

"Settle in, Jackie," I continued. "After all, you'll get a nice vacation with lots of meds and a nice padded white room and those paper-thin gowns with your ass out. And you'll get this walk, that sound everyone knows, that shuffle of your feet. Only very few people will know the truth. The Zodiac Killer lives in your body. You are the Gemini, my sweet love, Jackie. Feel me, Jackie. I'm alive. You're the one behind bars now, tape across your mouth.

Your dreams of the old insane asylum, that name tag around your wrist? It's all you, Jackie. It was your psychic premonition of what was to come. Now we'll always be together. How cozy . . . and every night I can crawl up next to you, inside of you. No one will listen. No one will care. You're safe with me now. You're a killing machine, and very soon your hands will be as dirty as mine."

I struggled to get louder, trying to drive Eddie's voice out of my head, staggering around on the sidewalk. I didn't even care who saw anymore. I had to get him out. I saw the station on Forty-Third and had the hope that I could run in there and yell, "I'm the next Zodiac Killer, and I need to be stopped!"

His voice came through my head like a lion's roar. "No, you don't! Not yet, not so fast. First you have to feel the lust of murder, the rush, the thrill. I'm not done yet." We fought, yelling at each other. I clutched my head and tried to make my voice—Jackie's voice—as loud as his. But I couldn't.

I stopped her yelling and looked around, forcing Jackie into the background, where she belonged. And what did I see standing in front of me but cartoons. Two fuckers dressed up in knockoff Elmo and Minnie Mouse costumes. Trying to get tourists to pose with them for a few bucks. And they were in my way. I pushed past, and one of them protested.

"Hey, who are you supposed to be?" Elmo asked my masked self. I went up to him and whispered into his mask where his ear would be, "Your worst fucking nightmare." I saw right through his costume to the young man whose face showed that he knew the devil had just spoken to him. He backed up and grabbed Minnie's hand.

I saw them as lovebirds getting shot dead. No, better yet, cut up and left on the corner for all to take pictures with. Oh, the news headlines would read, "Disney Gets Cut Up in Little Pieces." I was like a child in a candy store. So much to choose from. And I was doing it all for you, Jackie, my Gemini.

I moved through the crowd, looking for my dinner. Who shall stray into my path? Behind me, I heard a commotion. I turned and saw that Will person coming toward me, pushing people out of his way. I had to get away from him to complete my transformation and accomplish my mission. I moved like a pro on the football field as I dodged the crowds and ran away from him toward the West Village.

I turned down a dark city block and saw an old homeless man asleep against a building. A shopping cart full of his pathetic life was next to him as he lay covered by a filthy old blanket. I kicked his half-busted shoe. "Hey, drunk," I growled at him.

That's when my anger surfaced. Eddie always picked on the helpless. On the lost, the left behind, the ones most easily hurt. The ones who befriended me all my life. I pushed that anger forward and spoke in my own voice. "Don't hurt him! Leave him alone!"

"Why?" Eddie replied. "Because the old hobos on those

railroad tracks were the only ones that accepted you, you pathetic, motherless child." He bent down toward the man, who was now awake. "After tonight, everyone will know who you are. Get up, old man, I have a gift for you!"

"No!" I screamed. A hand was trying to remove the mask, but it wasn't mine. I wanted that damn mask off, but not if it was going to harm someone else, so I struggled to keep the mask on. "Don't take it!" I yelled at the poor man, whose face was frozen in fear as he started to crawl away from the possessed person. He said what I felt when he screamed, "Help me, God!"

Eddie yelled out and threw my arms wide, like he was nailed to a cross. One arm swung toward me and hit me on the head, and I started to feel faint. I couldn't fall now. "God, please help me," came out of my mouth in a mixture of two voices.

The homeless man, who had made it to a doorway and pulled himself up to a standing position, began to pray. In an instant, I pulled off the mask and fell to the ground. In my own quivering voice, I said, "Don't come near me. Stay back." I tried to look at the man, but one of my eyes was closed in pain, and the other made everything seem like I was seeing through a fish-eye lens.

I heard footsteps pounding up from behind me. It was Will. I held up the mask and begged him to take it. He stuffed it into his back pocket and picked me up.

He carried me across the street and looked into my eyes as they began to clear. My sight was spotted and hazy, but it was mine again, not Eddie's. Will wiped blood from my face and covered me with his coat.

The homeless man came over and put an old, broken string of rosary beads in my hand. "She saved my life," he told Will, as he wrapped my fingers tightly around the beads.

Will shifted, and a large knife fell out of my jacket pocket. Will snatched it away and put it into his own pocket. "Don't put that knife near that mask," I whispered into his neck as he held me. "Don't do it."

The homeless man gaped at me. "Look," he said, pointing at my face. "Her eyes, they're changing. She had one black eye . . . completely black . . . no whites, no pupil. Just a big, black hole. Now they're both sky blue." Just then, a drop of blood fell from that eye. It was Eddie, leaving my body.

The sweet man asked if we should call an ambulance. Will shook his head. "This isn't medical, my friend. It's spiritual." It certainly was. And as Will held me on that city street, I knew that every fire I walked through, he would be right there with me. I had known him before, I knew him now, and I would know him forever.

I don't know how we got home that night. I just remember a fog like the kind that blows off the ocean covering the ground. I awoke in bed, with Will sitting by my side and a wet cloth on my head. He took the cloth off and kissed me. I looked over at my nightstand and saw the broken rosary beads. Be it in this world or the next, I hoped that one day I would see that homeless man again.

That day I regained my strength enough to go to the bank. I put on dark glasses to shield my still-sensitive eyes from the light and went with Will to the branch where we have a safe-deposit box. We took both masks. I don't know why I hadn't thought of putting them in the safe-deposit box before. Along with valuable jewelry, it was where I kept things I didn't want in my house. And I sure as hell didn't want these anywhere near me anymore.

We entered the private little room in the back and put both pieces in the box. As we left, the box shook and moved along the table. I jumped back and called for the bank attendant. We told her we were done and watched her carefully as she used her key in unison with Will's to lock the box away. I could tell that we made her nervous and uneasy, but at least the box did not move again.

She worked quickly and then ran up the steps ahead of us. As we left, I stopped to tie my shoe, as the lace had come undone on the stairs. As I tied, I overheard her whispering to a coworker, "Those people gave me the creeps. The room turned ice cold, and I felt sick." As I straightened up, Will and I looked at each other. Will squeezed my hand and told me he loved me. We walked back into the sunlight knowing that the war was not over but that we had at least won a battle.

On the way home, I decided to take a detour. I suddenly felt the need to go to church. I wanted to confess the murderous thoughts I'd had in my head last night. I wanted to confess what Eddie had made me think. Will took a seat in a back pew to wait, and I walked into a confessional booth. Although I'm a religious person, we're not much for going to church—I believe God lives in every person, in the human soul, not just in buildings—

so going to confession was a very unusual thing for me. But then, so was walking the streets of Manhattan hoping to kill someone. So, I thought, why not?

The priest walked into his side of the confessional, and I kneeled down. "Father, I have a confession. Something got in me and I thought of murder—" He interrupted me by striking a match. A puff of cigarette smoke wafted through the mesh screen between us.

I knew immediately that this was not going to go as planned.

"Well, my child. Did you feel good? Or did you deny yourself?" he asked. His face pressed against the screen as I heard his pants unzip. He jerked back and forth. My hand went slowly to the doorknob but my eyes stayed on him. As I watched, his face became a demon—the wet, gray skin; the sharp features; a crusty substance in the corners of his mouth. He looked like a corpse. "You're right, Jackie, you're never alone. And this place is solace for all. It wouldn't exist without me. Now come and sit on my lap. Let me impale you. Touch me, Jackie."

I threw open the door on my side and yanked open the door on his. A priest sat there who looked nothing like what I had seen through the mesh screen. Startled, he jumped up and demanded I remove myself from the house of God. I backed away and looked around the church. All of the statues seemed to be grinning. The devil could find me anywhere. I could lock him away in one place, and he would come after me in another. I felt very tired.

FOURTEEN

Every night now, I prayed for sleep. It had been more than two and a half years since Patricia first thrust herself into my life. My body was tired and worn, my eyes heavy, my thoughts scattered. I was holding on to a thin thread of sanity, and I knew it could snap—*I* could snap—at any time. I was at the point where I looked forward to exhaustion, hoping for that kind of deep, heavy sleep. Maybe then I wouldn't remember any details that would affect my waking hours. Maybe then I wouldn't remember the nightmares.

One night, when I closed my eyes and drifted off to sleep, I found myself inside what looked like an abandoned warehouse, with dusty floors and shattered windowpanes. I could hear the wind blowing but couldn't feel it touch my skin. I walked slowly toward the center of the room and felt like I had passed an invisible line.

One step: nothing.

Two steps: the same.

Three steps: I'm not alone.

Four steps: I'm home.

And the room came to life. Or should I say death?

I saw two rows of white candles, making a perfect circle. Their flames swayed in unison. I stood just outside the ring of fire. And then that ancient book of spells slid out from a dark corner along the concrete floor and hit my bare foot. The candles flared, making the dark shadows around the circle dance fiercely. The book opened with a fury, and pages marked with the devil's ink flew out. Encrypted letters, symbols of the zodiac, the sign of the Gemini traced in blood—a scrapbook of murder and mutilation. The pages steadied themselves like a magic carpet would and then launched forward onto the walls around the flaming circle. I heard moans of ecstasy mixed with the sounds of a woman gurgling and choking on her own blood.

The walls turned to silken curtains, and I saw the tall man in black emerge slowly from behind them, directly across the circle of candles from me. He was dressed as usual, his hair perfect, his eyes like lit coals. As though performing a twisted striptease, he first poked one booted foot and a bloody knife into view, then stretched his arm out and made a fist. I could hear the leather of his gloves crackle.

"I am the Lord of Death, and this is your party. I will swallow your sins, Jackie, and drink from your throat, banishing you from this world once again." The book pages on the walls fluttered as he spoke. "You stand upon the burial grounds of the crossroads. The night belongs to me. Your name has been written on my arrow, spelled out *e-n-e-m-y*. You can't stop what has been prophesied. Satan's powers!"

I was unable to move or speak. He walked through the candle fire, disturbing not a single flame. He stopped in the middle of the circle and drew his mask out of a back pocket. He threw it on the floor and asked me if I liked to watch. I still couldn't speak.

He turned from me and began to slowly dance in place, now holding something in his arms. I could see a blood-stained sheet—a body wrapped up, the arms and feet dangling out, lifeless. I caught a glimpse of the head and knew then that it was a woman. He saw that I had seen, and the evil laughter roared from his mouth like a lion. He laughed and he danced, dragging her body around and around like a rag doll.

I could not turn away. I kept looking and saw a flash of something on her foot. It was a toe tag, the kind used on bodies in a morgue. I squinted, but the flickering candlelight and his quick movements made it impossible to read. He laughed at me again.

"You're trying to read the name, aren't you?"

He dropped the limp body on the ground, leaped to my edge of the circle, and grabbed me by the neck. He shoved the tag in my face and ordered me to read it.

Jane. Jackie. Patricia.
DOA.

The limp body on the floor changed from a woman to a child. And then, in a flash, I was that body, wrapped in the bloody sheet and held in his arms. I looked outside the circle and saw two little girls sitting there. One was me, the child Jackie, the girl I had been when I died on the operating table, my Forever Guardian. The other wore a yellow raincoat. They both moved as if to flee.

"Run!" I screamed at them. "He's going to kill you!"

"I already did." His fetid breath overwhelmed me as he whispered in my ear. "You can come back, and so can I. You'll never find that escape hatch, those golden gates to heaven. You're in my world now."

His world glowed and crackled with fire. But over the flames, I began to hear a low growl, coming from beyond the circle. He dropped me like I was nothing but a bag of bones and turned. The growl became a roar, and then its owner broke through the ring of fire and attacked. The beast ripped into the devil's arms as candles went flying everywhere, setting the walls on fire. I tried to escape, but the inferno was too great. I heard the devil scream.

"I'll be back, you damn bitch. There is only so much you can eat and take in, Jackie, before you explode or become one with me."

I knew what he meant. My work has always involved taking in evil from others in order to free them. It was finally catching up to me. The flames were getting closer.

But instead of heat, I felt coolness. The beast was beside me, licking me and jumping like a long-lost dog come home. And he had. It was my spirit guide, the Blackfoot wolf spirit assigned to me at birth. His painting hung on my bedroom wall, and I often spoke to him about the lost souls I encountered in my work.

He moved slightly and I saw the leather cord around his neck, partially hidden in his thick, gray fur. It was the one my father's father—the great medicine man—had used to put my mojo bag around my own neck.

I had not been forsaken. Thank God. I quickly grabbed the cord from around the wolf's neck. I knew to hold on and jump with him out of this nightmare. We leaped together, and I awoke back in my own bed. In my hands, I clutched my mojo bag, which I had certainly not taken to bed earlier. I sat up in bed and smiled at my wolf painting on the wall. The painted wolf's head seemed to tilt and his eyes to glow. We had made it back. Things were going to be all right. I tossed back the covers and swung my bare feet onto the floor. Something tugged at my toes and I looked down. A thin, yellowed cord was knotted tightly around my big toe. I swore and tried to pull it off, but it would not come untied. I raced to the kitchen and dug in a drawer for the scissors. They worked, thank goodness, and I pushed the cord into the sink garbage disposal—which was the nearest thing I could find—and ran water to flush the cursed thing away.

My rare moment of peace was gone. The exhaustion from my night of terror hit me hard. The smell of rotting death remained in my nose and worked its way down into my throat. I ran for the bathroom and leaned over the toilet, trying to cough it all up. Nothing happened, and the taste in my mouth grew worse. I went to the sink, grabbed my toothbrush, and went at my teeth as hard as I could. Foamy paste-and-blood bubbles swirled down the drain as I spit and rinsed. My smile was now white and shiny, but I knew as I stared at my sorry self in the mirror that it was only a superficial cleansing. The evil was still there.

I stopped trying to smile. The minute I closed my lips, the blood came back, tasting metallic in my mouth. My lower teeth felt tight, like there was something caught in them. I pulled a small flashlight out of my vanity and used the beam to see back toward my molars. I spotted what looked like a piece of bloody floss—but I had only brushed, not flossed! I grabbed the end and pulled to get it out from between my teeth, and the pain hit me like a shock wave. What the hell?

Dazed by the pain, I turned away from the mirror—and there she was. My roommate. My soul sister. My dead partner.

"Let's see, Jackie," Patricia giggled as she moved toward me.

I covered my mouth with one hand and pushed her with the other, yelling, "You're crazy! Leave me alone!"

She slapped my hands away. "How dare you call me crazy! I'm not going back to that nuthouse, not without you!"

She smacked my hand away from my mouth and with the strength of ten men—or one crazy dead lady—pulled my mouth open. Her gray fingers had bits of flesh missing and cracked brown nails. I gagged as she forced them into my mouth and began to pull. She shouted out with success as I felt her grab the floss. I stopped struggling and stood still in the hope that would end this whole thing more quickly. Our eyes met, and for a split second, I saw empathy in the black holes where hers had once been. Maybe it was for me; maybe it was for herself.

Then the rage returned and she gave a tremendous yank. The pain blew through me as she held up what she had ripped from my mouth. It wasn't floss at all. It was the cord. From the toe tag. Blood dripped from my mouth as if I'd gotten socked in the face. I clutched my jaw and felt a tooth wiggle back and forth.

Naturally, Patricia thought this was funny. She shook the bloody cord in my face. "You tried to eat your death away," she laughed.

That did it. I lunged for her. We pushed and shoved in my tiny bathroom, twisting and turning until I pinned her against the sink. I was facing the mirror and her back was reflected in the glass. I saw my face and the back of what was supposed to be her neck. But it was my neck, complete with my tattoo, a representation of my voodoo spirit doll that protects me—what I don't see coming, it will.

Well, I hadn't seen that one coming at all. Damn. I turned Patricia around slowly so that we both faced the mirror. We both looked like me. We had on the same clothes, same hair, same face. I was the only one bleeding, though. And her expression was different. I was out of breath. She was calm and studying me.

I swung her back around toward me and yelled, "What do you want from me?"

"I want to live," she yelled back.

No way. I pushed her away, and she hit her back against the sink counter. She didn't flinch, but I felt a sharp pain in my spine. I quickly realized that anything I did to her would only hurt me. We were becoming one. We faced off, staring at each other—or rather, I stared at myself.

"Get out, or I will cut you out," I finally shouted.

She retreated into the corner, her eyes still locked with mine, and turned back into the dead woman with her gray skin and stringy hair.

"My name is Patricia," she whispered. "Someone killed me, and no one cares."

What was I going to do? My heart ached for her.

"You care, Jackie," she pleaded. "We can live together, go out and get guys . . ."

And then she threw in stuff like that, wanting me to live her freewheeling, party-heavy lifestyle. I pulled my own hair in frustration. She grabbed her head in pain. Well, at least it went both ways. I forced my thoughts to a stop. What was I doing? Trying to hurt a ghost? Trying to reason with a vision? I was losing my mind. This wasn't real. I pushed past her and ran into my bedroom. She followed me, leaped onto my bed, and started tossing a red ball into the air like a child.

"Where did you get this?" I grabbed the ball from her.

"Stop yelling at me," she pouted.

"Patricia, where did you get this from?" I got in her face. "I need to know."

She stuttered as she backed away from me. "A little girl gave it to me. I see her, too."

What?

"You know, she was killed, too," Patricia said. "She told me so. Yep, she told me so. She whispered it right in my ear. A man killed her."

As she spoke, her words seemed to get further and further away, like they were echoing in my empty tunnel. My vision blurred, as though I were looking through a kaleidoscope, and in the middle stood this child in a yellow raincoat . . . waving . . . blowing out candles on a birthday cake . . . waving again . . .

The kaleidoscope twisted and the picture changed . . . a man now, dragging her away . . . tiny cries piercing my ears . . . the man, dropping her somewhere in the woods . . . turning toward me . . . closer and closer. Tilting his head from side to side and then squatting down, looking directly into the kaleidoscope lens at me . . . laughing . . . *I see you, too.*

I backed away and slapped my hands over my eyes. I sat down on my bed, next to Patricia, who hadn't moved while I saw those things.

I lost my temper. "God, make this stop."

She leaned toward me. "God wasn't home that night I was killed."

FIFTEEN

Going beyond the grave is as natural to me as drinking a glass of water. I can't get away from it, even when I try. And I have tried. But it is always the living who pull me back to death. People from all over the world, with all different educational levels and beliefs, all come to me for answers. The letters and the phone calls are relentless. There are always those who need me, either to help them communicate with a deceased loved one or to figure out their own past lives. And the spirits are just as persistent. Always tugging at my mind. There is only so much that a sponge can absorb before it needs to be wrung out and set aside to dry. I never get that chance. I don't know what it's like *not* to be soaked with other lives.

I also take away the demons. And I do mean that literally. My home has been used to expel countless entities. I take them in and pack them away so they can't escape. But the residue always remains. No matter how tightly you lock the box, the foul demon has seen your face and knows your home. I used to move often. My places would become so crowded that the knocks and bangs never stopped.

People send me cursed objects from all over the world for safekeeping. I store them securely, but they don't go away completely. Sometimes, when I am with a client, one of those demon boxes begins to bang. The poor person is always so startled, and I play it off—just a little activity stirring, nothing to worry about. What I really want to say is that I'm used to those damn demons trying to distract me. But they can't. They're not *my* demons. I can keep them in line. I am perfectly able to turn back to my clients and focus on their questions.

But now, I was the one who needed someone like me. I was the one who couldn't figure it out. Who does this child belong to? Why do I keep seeing her? What does she want from me? What is her message? I had stopped myself countless times from using my own skills to find the answers. I don't know why. Maybe it was the fear of knowing the truth. Maybe it was the fear of seeing things I would have no control over.

If I did do this, there would be no one to filter my discoveries. When I work with other people, I can tell them about their past lives in a gentle manner. I do not share the pictures of torture and death. I would not want anyone to relive such hideous acts. I take extreme care to never cross that line. But I could not offer that kindness to myself. I knew I would see the violence and death. Even though I had not gone there—yet—I was damn sure it was not a peaceful ending.

I had fought with myself for months, as this child's visits became more frequent. Now I sat in my office and finally decided that I would do it. I drew a chalk circle about five feet wide in the center of the room and then prepared two candles. The white one, I bathed with a homemade blend of oils called "in one with the spirit talks." The black candle I soaked with "the gate opener," an old recipe that has been in my family for generations. I needed to open the past in order to heal the future. It would not be nice to witness, but then death never was.

I washed my feet with holy water, which would take off the residue of any unwanted malevolent creatures of the night. Be gone, unclean spirits! I placed small mirrors in the circle—one in front of me and one behind—as well as my father's rain stick and my childhood music box, where a tiny ballerina spun slowly to Beethoven's *Moonlight Sonata*.

Summonings can be dangerous to perform. They tend to attract a few hitchhikers, little entities that slip quickly through, trying to find a home for haunting in a dark corner or in a weak person. These beings are built for destruction and will definitely make your life hell. I can shoo them away, but I still have to keep my guard up.

I hung my mojo bag around my neck. Then I picked up my chalk again and drew the symbols that represent the gods of aid in Native American beliefs. I moved in the ritual dance of the dead, which shows allegiance and honor. The spirit shall carry on.

When I had finished drawing the symbols, I read from an old book of psalms, my voice rising louder and louder as the summoning began. The chandelier above me started to sway and the bulbs to flicker. Light bounced off the walls, and the air became thick and still. The smell of freshly turned earth rose from the floor. The dead walked alongside me now.

"Come forward, child." I spoke as I sat and began rocking back and forth. "Come forward and speak to me."

The candle flames shot up and then blew out. The music box stopped. The floor began to creak and then, in the far corner of the room by the door to the laundry room, was the image of this little girl. I dropped the Book of Psalms and leaned forward.

"Who are you?" I asked gently. "Why are you always with me? Why do I know you?"

I stared into the dark corner. She had her face to the wall. Small cries, like a dove in distress, came from her. And then, a soft voice.

"I was never supposed to interfere with the person I am now. My body is in heaven. My spirit is you."

I sat back, shocked. It was true. I had tried for so long to convince myself otherwise. I had been in denial. *I* couldn't have ever been a victim. I was the person other people came to for justice! I helped others deal with *their* deaths. How the hell was I supposed to help myself? How could I get past the feeling of my own killer's hands around my throat?

"You are to avenge the broken wings of innocence," she said to me. "I know who I went into at birth, and you saw me, too. For all the people young and old, it is you who shall attract the monster, rid them."

This little girl in a yellow raincoat named Jane was me in a previous life. And her choosing to be reincarnated as me was no mistake. She knew that if anyone could get justice and exact vengeance, it was the daughter of a medium and a medicine man. I could not speak. Pictures of this child's murder played in my mind. I jumped up in horror, instinctively trying to get away, and my foot accidentally went through the chalk line and broke the circle. I searched frantically for the chalk—I knew that with the circle open, I was exposed to the dark elements and in great danger. I saw it rolling across the floor, spinning quickly out of my reach as though pulled by an invisible force.

The laundry room door banged open, and Patricia's voice yelled for the child to run. The girl took off like dust in a windstorm. The door slammed shut, and she was gone. That corner of the room plunged into black. And then, barely, he moved. The tall man in black crouched down to mimic the height of the child. He hid his face with his arm, and spoke to me in a child's voice.

"Let's play a game . . . I'll count. One . . . two . . ."

His long combat knife slid across the floor and into my broken circle. The handle hit my leg.

"Three . . . pick it up."

I sat still.

"Four . . ."

My hand shook uncontrollably as I tried to stop myself from reaching toward it.

"Nine . . ."

"Stop!" I yelled. "You can't go from four to nine! Stop!"

He was still using her little-girl voice.

"Pick it up and slit your throat."

I closed my eyes and told myself that this was not real. The next thing I knew, he had crawled over to me—into my broken circle, damn it—and grabbed my hands.

"It is real. It's all real." His grip hurt. "Look at me, Jackie. Don't you believe in God? Isn't that what you preach? What would God be without me?"

His fingers were like iron on mine.

"Now, we don't need you knowing too much. Pick up that knife before I do."

I took the knife, and his eyes gleamed with victory.

"I knew you would, Jackie. Put it to your throat. Let me eat your sins away. It won't hurt."

I stared into his eyes. His words were hypnotic. I began to forget my own existence, as though a huge eraser were wiping away my memory. I felt lost. I was close to death, close to taking my life at his command. And then something came over me. It was a rage and a love all at once. I remembered who I was. I was loved. I was needed. And I fought this kind of evil. I would fight it now with its own weapon.

I turned the knife into this rotten thing that slinks from prison and finds its next victim, then slithers back in glory, slapping God in the face. I leaped toward him and shoved the knife deep into his gut.

He just looked at me, and then we both looked at his stomach, where there was no wound and no blood. He fell, laughing and holding his middle. "Ohhhh, she killed me . . ." He rolled on the floor, still laughing.

I had to do something. I grabbed one of the mirrors and held it up to him, to show the devil his own face. He knocked it out of my hands.

"Jackie, you're a killer, just like me. You plunged that knife in so hard, so good. You made me proud. How did it feel, Jackie? Better than sex?" He laughed in my face. "You can't kill what's already dead."

He walked through my broken circle, kicking over my religious relics, and sat in my office chair. He leaned back and nonchalantly rolled a smoke. I knew what he was doing—reliving Eddie's actions years later. The killing man.

"Hey, Jackie. You're supposed to ask me if I got a smoke." He held up the cigarette as though he were enticing me over. I did not move from where I'd pressed myself up against the wall on the other side of the room.

"Come over to me, Jackie. Let's take a walk in the park."

I still didn't move.

"Take this!" He jumped toward me. "It's what you wanted, remember, Patricia?"

I took it. He lit it. I smoked it.

"You're a sinner, Jackie."

The sound of my inhale was drowned out by the garage door opening. Will was home. He would come through the laundry room door any second.

"I am always with you," he hissed.

Will opened the door and there was only me, standing against the wall, smoking a cigarette. He looked at the scattered relics and smudged chalk.

"You doing a ritual or something? Who were you talking to? I heard a man's voice."

He wanted my husband to think I was crazy. He would be back.

The house phone rang upstairs, and we both ran up the steps. It was the prison. My finger automatically accepted the call by pushing number 3.

"Hi, Jackie, this is Eddie. Did you see it?" He was excited, I could tell.

"Yes, I saw. Eddie, what made you kill?"

His excitement came through the phone line.

"It's a long story that's unfolding for your eyes only . . . God and the devil are sitting at a big table. God tells the devil, 'Move forward and be known.' And I was born." He chuckled. "Be careful, Jackie," he said sarcastically, "so it doesn't jump into you."

Eddie kept calling me from prison. We had been having phone conversations for more than a year now, and of course, Patricia had used me to contact him even before that. I was pretty much the only human being he talked to. Sometimes we would just chat about mundane things. He told me what he ate, how he was feeling, what other prisoners were located in cells near to his own. He was housed by himself, and he liked it that way. He had no problem being alone with his thoughts. His cell was about eight and a half feet long and six feet wide, and his bed was a concrete slab covered with a thin mattress.

Other times, he would bring up other subjects. "Jackie,

you listened to the newspapers when they ran my story, to all the movies, to experts on me and others just like me. Now listen to me. I am the Zodiac. They think it's safe. The public can sleep. How wrong are they . . .

"I have taught you about weapons. How I work alone in the dark. Studying the prey, developing my skills. I can easily leave and transform into anything." Now it was my job to find him, he told me. He could change his color or his gender, but I would find him because his eyes— those all-black orbs—would always be the same.

"You're different. The others don't see me coming. You not only see me but feel my blood begin to pump; my mouth begin to water. The taste of blood, the feel of it on my skin, moving my tongue over my teeth. The stench of death that surrounds me could never be washed away. You'll look in the mirror and see me . . . You'll feel me touch your skin, that old familiar that I am now. When I take a deep breath, I can smell you. When I close my eyes, I can pull your body in. When I speak, I can sound just like you."

He loved taunting me. "What are you going to say? 'Hello, 911, the Zodiac Killer is able to move from person to person. He's haunting me.'" And he was right. What would I say to people who lived only in the "normal" world? People who couldn't see? He knew—and I knew— that the only time most people questioned these types of things was when a seemingly normal person went on a senseless rampage. There was no rhyme or reason for who the devil picked to live in, he told me. I knew that, too.

On the surface, Eddie was not one of those normal

people anyway. He'd had a rough upbringing—no father in his life; a childhood in a bad, drug-infested neighborhood; very little education. There were reasons and rationales for why he had become such a killer. But then, there were the other things, things a bad childhood certainly couldn't explain. How did someone with practically no formal education and a technically low IQ teach himself how to assemble guns and make bullets? And how did he know about things like the occult when—back in the days before the Internet—such subjects were almost impossible to learn about without being part of an established occult group? He didn't learn any of these things on his own, that's how. He had his devil twin to help him.

Eventually, Eddie told me about what he considered to be his masterwork, his murder of Patricia. Over several days, he relived how he'd killed her, savoring both the details of the crime and how much hearing them hurt me. Patricia was an unwanted presence in my life, sure, but I knew she was a victim, and to hear how she had died was excruciating for me. I kept him talking, though, because I thought it was important for people to know exactly what he had done and what he was thinking while he did it. About the night he became the soul collector.

It was nighttime in the park. The wind blew through the trees. People walked around, lovers kissed. He knew exactly where to wait. He had waited two years since his last attack, and now it was time. He told himself to get ready. Here she came. Don't move too fast, steady yourself. Look at her.

He could tell she had nothing, was nothing. Talking to herself every few seconds. The filth had no bra on, swinging her hips, trying to get fucked. She made him sick. He licked his lips and moved around the bushes to watch her in her tight pants. He could see her nipples through her black T-shirt, which had a flower design on the front. Flowers, which laid on her like she was in a coffin, like when they place a bouquet over a body's chest. He was her undertaker, coming to collect her body. His sweet, dear little sinner. She wanted him to fuck her.

He crept a little closer and she felt him. He smiled. He heard her ask someone for a smoke. He quickly rolled a piece of paper as though it were a cigarette and held it up enough to catch her eye. He had her now. He turned and walked ahead of her, his heart beating with joy. He didn't even have to turn around. He knew she would follow.

She did, and his joy grew, but then she spoke. He hated that. He never wanted his kills to speak.

"Why don't you stop walking? Where are you taking me?" she said.

He looked back. Just a little bit farther. She climbed the steps after him, her breasts jumping up and down as she tried to keep up. He reached into his back pocket, took out his ski mask, and put it on. She told him she thought it was sexy.

"Do you like me? Do you want me?" She was trying to turn him on. Come closer. She did and tried to take what she thought was the smoke. She rubbed herself on him, but he wasn't hard from that. He was hard from the thought of his next move. He pushed her away slightly, backing her up to get a good shot.

"I like you so much, I'm going to keep you forever."

She saw the gun and said, "No, please." He felt his eyes roll back in his head and his belly begin to fill. He shot her and she went down. He waited for her to die, because only then could he collect her soul. But she did not. She struggled and fought to get up. Silly girl. He shot her again. She fell again but kept trying to drag herself away from him. How dare she try to get away from her god!

He wanted to see the panic in her eyes, so he got down on his belly beside her and crawled along with her. She kept begging him, but that only turned him on more. That was when he decided that he needed to feel his knife plunge into her, so he could hear the sound of it piercing her flesh.

He pinned her down and slowly licked both sides of the knife blade. She tried to shield her face with her arms, and he laughed at her. As if that would stop him. He plunged the knife in . . . so many times he lost count. It felt so good, he couldn't stop. When he was finally done, he lay beside her and looked at his treasure. She was drenched in her own blood.

But not a drop had touched him. He watched her life run out—those last breaths were always so satisfying. He wanted nothing more than to lay beside his bride, his child, his best kill, his everything. He had waited so long for the perfect one. He saw his breath, despite the August heat, and wiped his mouth as he stretched out next to her, his other half that he would keep forever. He wanted to collect her soul and share their togetherness. Such a sweet moment, he thought.

She had only just begun to live under his thumb, to be his

eternal and ever-after slave. He would never be hungry
again. She filled his gut. He lay there and thought.

I am humanity.

I am tranquility.

I am the ocean, the sky.

I am your tears.

I am the brother of man—the other brother.

I am the air on your cheeks.

I am your last drop of blood.

Even though the park was full of homeless people and
druggies, he and she were alone. He felt light-headed as he
looked at his knife, still shiny with blood. He felt like it was
Christmas morning, and he had just gotten the toy he'd
been wanting all year. But now he had to get home. He
wiped off the knife and put it in his jacket pocket, along with
his mask.

He left the flesh behind for the pig cops to find and walked
quickly out of the park—not because he was afraid of getting
caught, but so that he could get home to be with his newly
collected soul. He passed by people who all seemed to race by
as though they couldn't see him. Figures and faces he couldn't
make out flashed by as a voice inside told him how good he
had done.

He closed the door to his room and put his gun and the
knife in his desk drawer. He changed his clothes and jumped
into bed, smelling the blood on a rag he held. Then he made
love to his kill. Not the body, but the soul. He felt her next
to him. So exciting.

He got up and looked at his body. He let his hand run
over his chest. He had done it.

I accomplished it. I am the Zodiac.
The higher beast.
The hunger.
The hunter.
The master.

I thought Eddie telling me all this was a one-way confessional, but he did not want to play that way.

"Jackie, I have been meaning to ask you something."

"What?" I said.

"Tell me what happened to you at age eight. Do you remember yet?"

"A lot happened to me," I said quietly.

"Do you see it?" he pressed further. "Can you tell me?"

I heard a guard in the background yell for him to hang up the phone.

"Ooops. I have to go, Jackie. Time is up. Session over." He paused. "Tomorrow, you get to lay on the couch, and I ask the questions. We'll play shrink . . ."

He laughed and hung up. I was left standing stunned in the middle of my kitchen. I had never mentioned my visions of Jane, never referred to reincarnation in any way.

He liked to shake me up. At the end of a different conversation, he told me that he sometimes sat in his cell and wondered what I was doing. "I stare at the ceiling and it begins to swirl around, like water, and I see you . . . I can see you . . ."

SIXTEEN

I had planned to have after-dinner coffee with a dear friend. As time rolled on, I kept trying for normalcy, so I made the plans days before. But instead of dressing to meet her, I put on a black hoodie and tucked a wrapped bundle into a tote bag. I walked down the West Side Highway, looking for a place to dump it. I heard people's thoughts as they walked past me. "What's with her face?" they asked themselves, unaware that I could hear every word. I kept searching and finally found a sewer. I threw the bundle down it as hard as I could, like I was afraid it would hurt me. "There," I said, "you can't kill me again."

I had just dumped every kitchen and utility knife from my house into the sewer. As I stared down the hole I came to myself, like a sleepwalker awakening to find herself in front of the refrigerator. I shook my head. I remembered the walk but had no idea where I was, which scared the hell out of me. I stopped a passerby and asked for directions to the subway. I felt like a child away from home and wanted to say, "Help me, I'm lost," but I kept my mouth shut.

I stumbled in the direction the man pointed me. I didn't know how long I walked before I passed a night club that had thumping bass coming from inside and two huge bouncers standing outside.

"Hey, Patricia, you coming in tonight?" one of them hollered at me.

What?

The other one scowled at me. "No drunken shit tonight. I'm not in the mood," he growled.

"I'm not Patricia," I stuttered. "That's not my name. You got the wrong person."

They laughed at me as I fled.

I found an all-night diner and stood outside, looking in at the light and the people. The activity made me feel less alone. I fumbled for my cell phone and tried to call Will. It didn't occur to me to call my friend and tell her I wouldn't be making our coffee date in a different part of the city. For a moment, I couldn't figure out what buttons to push. I finally succeeded, only to get his voice mail. I told him where I was and asked him to come pick me up, since I still had no idea how to get to the subway.

The diner seemed like a safe place to wait. It was crowded with late-night customers, many of them laughing as they relived their nights out on the town. They ignored me as I walked past on my way toward the one empty booth in the back. I sat down and cradled my pounding head in my hands.

"Well, are you going to just sit there? I don't have all day. What can I get you?"

I looked up to see an older woman, with curly red hair and flaming lipstick to match. Her face was lined with what I was sure were her own heartaches as well as the weary work of tending to hungry drunks on the night shift. I asked for strong coffee and a menu in what I thought was a polite manner. She did not.

"One strong cup of piss and find me a menu," she yelled toward the kitchen. "We got a prima donna on our hands."

She stomped off, and I headed for the bathroom to wash up. I shouldn't have bothered. The place reeked, and since there were no paper towels, I ended up wiping my hands on my own shirt. Still rubbing them dry, I walked back to my booth to find someone sitting there, his back to me.

"Excuse me, this is my seat, and I'm waiting for someone," I said.

It was the tall man in black, immaculately dressed in a suit. He sipped a cup of coffee and told me to sit down.

He smiled at me. A perfect smile. "Come on, Jackie. Look around. This is New York City, the city that never sleeps." He gestured around him. "I know what you're thinking. What am I doing in a dump like this?" I didn't take my eyes off him. "It takes all walks of life. Some I know, some I'm waiting to be acquainted with. You know, Jackie, when they cross my path I'll be there for them. No sir, I will not let them down."

I stared at his face. This was the first time we had sat and had an actual conversation, so I took advantage of the opportunity to look at him without fearing for my life. His eyes were dark and intense and seemed to collect suffering. He reached over the table and grabbed my hand. I barely noticed the waitress bring my coffee.

"Jackie, I'm everywhere. I made history many times. I collect what is left over . . . Look at it like this. Credit me for your existence."

What?

He tilted his head as if he were examining me for a crack he could use to get in. "Why, if it wasn't for me, who would you be? I made you who you are. I put you on the map . . . Oh, Jackie, don't look so confused. If evil didn't exist, how would the honorable become honorable?"

He pulled my hand closer to him, forcing me to look even more closely at him. I felt myself going into his world, being pulled into my psychic realm. I felt the change. Loud noise pierced my ears, and words started to echo in my skull.

"Jackie, look back over the counter at those cooks," he ordered me. I turned, and instead of the two ordinary men sweating behind the grill I had noticed earlier, I saw a large man in a clown suit throwing together a ham sandwich. His stained gloves slapped down each slice of meat with a thump. He was standing next to a well-groomed, handsome man with dark hair. They were comparing notes.

The clown bragged—he'd strangled, mutilated, tortured. The other one grinned. "At least I wasn't a faggot, getting off on handcuffed guys."

"Yeah, well, I fooled everyone," the clown said. "I had them all under my own house. Their own little graveyard. I was a well-respected part of society. I had them all fooled."

"Well, I had the brains," said the handsome one. "I became that lawyer, even representing myself. I got up in court and stood near that jury and questioned that pig of a detective, made him even explain in detail what he saw—not leaving anything out. I was hungry for the kill, and it got me off. Better than sex!"

They went on, talking and laughing. My companion tugged at my hand to bring my attention back to him. He knew whom I had seen, since he was the one who showed them to me. He was making a point. *Look at the soldiers in my army. Eddie isn't the only one.* "You can wipe them off the earth but never clean away the acts. They live in my world and yours. Times change and others are born, giving me great joy." His grip tightened, and his feet curled around mine under the table. He knew I wanted to run. "I am the Zodiac. You looked for the truth and found me. How does it feel, Jackie, to be in my world?"

Sweat dripped down my face and stung my eyes. He noticed my untouched coffee and dumped sugar into it. Then he added cream. It hit the flat black surface and turned to blood. Red rippled through my cup. He stuck his finger in and slowly stirred. His booted foot rode up my leg and his eyes glinted with pleasure. He took his dripping finger out of the cup of gore and reached toward me, wiping it across my lips.

Unlike with some of his previous visits to me, this time

I knew I was in full psychic mode, and that no one else could see this tall man in black, this devil twin of Eddie. It wasn't real. But it *was* disgusting. I fought back the urge to gag.

"Take this, Jackie, and drink. This is my blood, the blood of sin and lust. The blood of evil. Be my Gemini. You will live forever in the heart and souls of the weak. You will finish my work of mass destruction, you have the unknown power. Lay with me by day and stalk by night. Look what God has put you through. Let me in . . ."

Enough. I jumped up, knocking over my coffee. There was no one across from me. The crowded babble of patrons returned to my ears. The cooks at the grill were two normal guys. The waitress stomped over with a soiled wet rag.

"What the hell does this look like, a fucking hotel? No sleeping in this joint. Come on, buy something or get going."

"No, no . . ." I pleaded. I tossed six bucks on the table in the hope that would calm her down and shut her up. I needed to get home, and Will hadn't come. I would have to find the subway on my own. Where was the R train? She laughed at me as I headed for the exit. "Looking for Bellevue, lady? Just keep going toward Broadway; you'll run into it."

Everyone heard that, and their stares followed me as I made my way awkwardly toward the door. As I opened it, I took a quick glance back. Were they still staring? Instead of a row of men at the counter, there now sat only a woman with a child—a little girl in a yellow raincoat. I looked at her, with her little legs dangling from the stool, and I remembered. I flashed back to when I was dragged away by a man. To choking for air as hands tightened around my neck.

I staggered outside, wheezing. I grabbed on to a pole just to stay upright. A man walked past, looking at me as if he thought I was just some common junkie in need of a fix. Then suddenly he stopped and came closer.

"It doesn't have to be like this," he whispered and then walked away. The devil had overtaken that ordinary man, just to show me how powerful he was. No matter where I went or how fast I ran away, the devil could enter anyone and find me at any time. I was never safe. I eventually made my way to the subway station, praying the whole way that I would wake up from this nightmare. Somehow, I made it home. Will, who had not gotten my message, was waiting for me outside.

"Where were you?" he said.

"Hell," I yelled. "I was in hell!"

"Jackie, look at me," he said. "You can't take the sins away from the world. You'll die."

"I already did, and I came back." I yelled, almost in spite of myself, as I raced into the house and up to the bathroom. All I wanted was to soak in a hot bath, to be one with myself, to not share my body with anything or anyone. I slid into the hot water and tried to wash away the filth. By the time I got out, Will was in bed, worn out from concern for me. All he could manage to say was good night. I slid into bed next to him and curled into a fetal position.

And then there was a hand over my mouth. My body was pulled by an invisible force. I felt his body next to mine and his arm around me. This tall man in black, the Zodiac.

"Come to me, Jackie. Listen to my voice. Feel me."

And I fell, farther and farther, down into darkness. I couldn't tell whether I was asleep, dying, or finally succumbing to his demands. And still I fell . . .

. . . I landed in what looked like the lobby of a hotel. A man rushed up and immediately shoved a small suitcase into my hands. He carried an identical one.

"Hurry, Patricia, no time to wait," he said as he guided me to the elevator. We rode upward until he ushered me off and over to room 810. He hurriedly pushed open the door and told me to take off my own clothes and put on what was in the suitcase.

The brass snaps on the suitcase popped as I opened it. I pulled out a drab-green hospital gown designed to tie in the back. He shook his head at me. "Tsk, tsk. Put it on open in the front," he said as he scurried around, getting things ready. I felt like I was late for a very important date.

He opened his own suitcase and began putting on medical scrubs and a cap. I followed his orders and pulled the gown's edges together, embarrassed.

"Nonsense," he chided. "The body is not the body; it's a learning tool."

He snapped on a pair of long black gloves. I could smell the heavy rubber. He impatiently turned down the bed and waved me toward it. I climbed in. The sun was so strong I could barely open my eyes. Instead, I used my ears and heard the sounds of metal objects clanging against one another. A microphone came on and amplified the man as he introduced himself to what sounded like a group of students. He explained what everyone was about to witness. And then I understood.

The sun was a large overhead lamp. The bed was a metal autopsy table with a drain. The pillow was a rubber block with a cutout to hold my neck in place.

"What we have here is a cadaver. A murder victim," the man intoned into the microphone. My robe was pulled open. I no longer cared. Modesty was no longer a virtue.

I lay there as he cut into me. His voice started to float away and other things started to float in. Bits and pieces. Numbers. Room numbers. Room 810. 8-10. The eighth month and the tenth day. August tenth, the date of my death.

"Cause of death—two gunshots and over a hundred stab wounds." He stuck his hands inside my opened body. I felt nothing. I was nothing but a slab of meat. My mind drifted away, back to times when I was happy. I had to go way, way back, that's for sure. Maybe when I was a teenager, when I would laugh as I ran around with my friends. I tried even further back, and earlier memories came closer, but the man's voice interrupted. He was still talking to his audience, and I could see him above me, pulling me apart.

He stopped talking and moved closer, staring at my face. Did he know I was still inside? That I was this corpse? Is this all there was? I felt tears fill my eyes and spill over onto my cheeks, one at a time. They were warm on my ice-cold skin. Did I get shock treatment and now was hallucinating? It could be. I could be alive. Or was that wishful thinking? The table was cold, and my life was oozing down its drain.

The man kept staring at my face. He grabbed the mic and told his students that it was only leftover fluid escaping from the tear ducts. But his look said something different. He knew. He put a damp cloth over my eyes. Was it because he knew I was still in here and he felt guilty about it? Or was it for me, so I wouldn't see my body getting carved up—again—and could go back to thinking about times when I was loved? Did he know how to move the soul out? Where would I go?

Time passed—I didn't know how much. Finally, I heard the metal table bang and tools being put back into place. I opened my eyes to find myself standing outside the same elevator, dressed in unfamiliar clothes. A child in a yellow raincoat stood next to me. She seemed very anxious to get where she was going.

When the elevator got there, she jumped on and waved me in with a smile. She knew more than I did. She'd done this before. I got on and looked at the buttons. As I moved to push one, she touched my arm.

"We don't have to do that. It knows where to take us. Just watch."

I looked down at her pure little face. Her eyes seemed to hold years of wisdom. Can an angel be this tiny and wear a yellow raincoat?

"Is it raining out?" I asked.

She looked down at herself. "No. I had this on when that bad man killed me. It doesn't rain anymore."

I couldn't believe what I was hearing.

"What's your name?" I asked her.

"Jane," she replied, and then bounced up and down on her little tiptoes. "I know your name."

"You do?" I said. Her tiny hand covered her mouth in delight. "Well, my name is Patricia, but all my friends call me Trish," I said.

She stared at me. "No . . . no. Your name is Jackie." She looked as though she had just spilled a secret. I couldn't think of what to say.

"No . . . my name is Patricia," I finally managed.

She kept looking at me, and I turned, looking everywhere but at her. I could see the sky through the vent in the ceiling. The buttons on the panel were all flashing. I punched one to stop the elevator.

"Don't do that. It's not going to stop until we're there," Jane said.

We rode in silence and then the elevator slammed to a halt. I grabbed on to her, trying to protect this kid as the elevator began to bend and turn like a Rubik's Cube. One twist. Two twists. Done. It was now a seat for two. A bar came down over our laps and locked into place.

"What is this?" I shouted. I felt our seat start moving down a track. "Let me out. Holy shit!"

Jane looked at me. "It's okay, Jackie."

My name was Patricia, but I didn't want to fight her on the name thing anymore. Call me what you want. I was just terrified of the roller coaster. I always had been.

"Look, kid. I can't do this. Don't you understand? I'm

scared. I can't do this. I would rather chase the devil . . ."
I said.

"You do, Jackie," she laughed, then said, "I want to
show you something."

"Jesus Christ, kid, I don't even know you," I yelled as
our seat picked up speed. I truly hated roller coasters.
"Hello! Anyone out there? Get me off this ride, now!"

We looked at each other, and I saw her good, maybe
for the first time. Real good. It was like looking in the
mirror as a kid, a fast glance at myself. I heard what
sounded like my dad call out, "Jackie." I shook my head,
trying to stop the sounds. That wasn't my name.

Jane raised her arms. "Now, don't forget to hold your
arms up and wiggle your fingers like this," she said.

I stared at her little face, all excited. My heart thumped
like a bunny's foot beating on the ground. Excitement
and nerves at the same time. She laughed at me, at us.
Our little seat coasted into a shed that had the controls.
A man came out. He was dressed in old-fashioned suspenders hooked to worn pants. His sleeves were rolled up,
and there was a top hat on his head. I could tell that his
boots had seen a lot of miles. Kind of like me.

He smiled at us, and it warmed my whole cold body.
I suddenly knew I was going to be okay.

"Jane," he said to the little girl. "I should have known.
You're a real firecracker. All right, come on now; give
us your tickets."

"Jacob," Jane said, all polite-like, "I'd like to introduce
you. This is Jackie."

He looked at her as he tore the tickets in half. "Yes, Jane, I know. Remember, it was my idea. You could have been anyone. It was my idea, Jane. I couldn't take away what happened, but I know how to get vengeance."

He tapped the brim of his top hat, and it sparkled as he touched it. Tiny twinkles and little stars bounced around, and microscopic golden butterflies danced in a halo around his head. *Oh my. If there was really a Santa Claus, it would certainly be him*, I thought. Even though he obviously had me confused with this Jackie person. My name was Patricia.

He knew what I was thinking, and a big smile crossed his face.

"Here you go," he said, handing us back our halves of the tickets. "Now, off . . . off . . . off . . ."

We sailed up and into the sky. I felt my heart drop, but it was wonderful, not scary. Wheeeee!

"Hold your hands up. Do it like this!" Jane lifted her little arms into the sky, full of blue, purple, and pink clouds. Swooping up and down, we screamed with joy. The twists and turns, her little face shining in the sun, rays of warmth on us. Touching us.

I wasn't cold anymore . . .

. . . Jane looked over at me and suddenly I felt like myself again. Like Jackie. Cold, cold Patricia was gone.

I turned toward Jane and the words came out before I knew I was going to say anything. "Your mother loved you, Jane. I'm sorry." I stopped myself before I could say the rest—that I was sorry Jane had come back as me.

"I know," she said and then turned and pointed over the side. "Look down, Jackie. Don't be scared."

As the roller coaster raced through the marshmallow clouds, I looked down and saw the big top of the circus. Thousands of children jumped and waved up at us. I heard the pipes of the organ. And then I saw a wolf, huge and gray, running on the ground below as though he were racing to meet us at the finish line.

We went through a tunnel so bright that it hurt my eyes, but it didn't appear to harm Jane's. She seemed to see perfectly. We came to a stop in the shed, and I saw that wolf guarding the entrance, to make sure I used the exit on the other side. I was not supposed to stay. The same man in the top hat was waiting for us. He smiled at Jane as if he had given her the gift of a lifetime. Or maybe two lifetimes. He took her hand and bowed, putting his top hat over his heart as he helped her out of our roller-coaster car. She looked back at me.

"You can't come. Not yet," she said. "Go back and help us."

"How, Jane?"

She began to fade and her voice sounded far away.

"By being who you are."

"Who am I, Jane?" I asked.

"A murdered child. Who came back."

SEVENTEEN

———

I sat on my bedroom floor with a little notebook. I had decided that I needed to get this all down. Some kind of explanation about what was taking over me. I was changing into something that science could not explain. The reflection I saw wasn't mine. My actions were shared with others. I was not alone, and I feared that I was fading away. Me, Jackie. And if I didn't make a record of it, no one would know. So I started to write, and the words that poured out came from me—and from Patricia . . .

> *It begins very slowly, a tiny tug that I shake off. Bumps and bangs in the dark, voices in my pillow, waking in different places. Now I say my name over and over just to confirm my own sanity.*
>
> *I lie in my bed, watching the walls turn to ash. The room closes in. The sounds of cruelty in my ears form a*

picture. For each vision, the painter adds to the masterpiece of horror that was this other person's life.

My body twists and turns with the unbearable physical and emotional pain. Doctors can't help—they haven't studied the other side yet. No one listens. Is this what it's like to be in a coma? Can anyone hear me?

Something is growing inside me. I see her, I act like her, walk different, talk different. Sometimes I am locked in the closet, where no one can hear me. My hands bleed from pounding on the door. The sounds get louder. I see the night in different shades, looking for the home she never had. She speaks to me while tracing a life with a thick black marker.

The demon also sees the marker and walks behind, every step of his big heavy boots leaving a trail of mayhem and murder. For the first time, I see and know my killer. My killer. The words can crumble the highest mountain, bring the strongest to their knees.

He climbs the tenement stairs, runs through the drug-infested hallways. Babies crying, people fighting, music blasting. He leaves drops of my life behind that will be stepped on by others, then mopped away. I stand in each stairwell corner, just watching. He has no regret. He just took me, wiped me out. As though I were trash.

I bow my head. If only my existence in this world had been different. The mental hospitals couldn't help me. The medicine didn't work. All that inhumane treatment . . . Did anyone care? My family . . . did I let them down? Was I ever loved? Will I be remembered?

His boots bang on every step. He can wash away the blood on his hands, but he can never wash away his actions. The monster in the flesh. I'm seeing a murder. I'm living his victim.

I long to be Jackie. My mind is cluttered with memories of death. Fears I never had before now consume me. I have outbursts of rage that only a victim would have. Or a person with schizophrenia. Sharing space in one body can't last long. My life has become a time bomb, ready to go off at any moment. After the smoke clears, I will be someone else.

I am being held by a serial killer. I am possessed by his victim and by a child who wants me to remember who I was.

Is this happening because somehow I pushed my work away and ignored the existence of pure evil? Am I being forced to face my faith? What is my purpose in life? What was her purpose in life? To suffer the torture of mental illness and die at the hands of a serial killer? The secret of that killer lies deep within me, put there by Patricia. I can smell him near. I walk through his room, the sick smell of his hamper of soiled clothes, my life staining them.

He runs to his book and takes notes of his work. Using the same hands that snuffed me out. He kneels beside his bed like a child would. "Dear Father . . . Now I lay me down to sleep, a hundred souls for me to keep. If I should die before I wake, I pray to God that soul I take! And mine is the kingdom and glory. Amen." He jumps into bed, a warm smile across his face. "I had my first girl. A hundred times." He chuckles . . .

All of this was in my head. I took the paper, now covered with my writings, and stuffed it between my mattress and box spring. So if I went away, it would be there to be found. It felt like a suicide note, and in some odd way, maybe it was. I felt like I was leaving and I wasn't sure if I would return.

My name is Jackie.

Even getting ready for the day had become a chore. Normal tasks, like brushing my teeth or taking a shower, would be interrupted by Patricia, with the tall man in black right at her heels. My heels.

This was not only making my personal life impossible, it was making my work much more difficult than it already was. My days were always packed with clients who needed my insight or guidance, who sought truth or spirituality in today's cynical world. We all need to return to what is real, restore our souls, put peace in our hearts. And none need this more than people on both sides of the divide caused by murder.

The crime files stacked on my desk weighed heavily on my heart. I would look at all the faces, gently rubbing their photos, consoling them. Then they would get individual containers, with small tokens of happiness around their files. I knew what each victim had liked in life and placed little keepsakes inside, along with fresh flowers. Then in would go the photos of happy times with their loved ones. I noticed long ago that survivors always sent pictures of the happy times, of their families together.

They wanted me to know the strength of their love, of course. And I always did.

But now, I needed a break from the desperate expressions of those left behind. I instructed Joanne not to book any homicide cases for the whole week. I just couldn't look at any more despair. And to be honest, I was afraid that this company of mine would awaken and frighten the hell out of these people who were already victims. I cringed at the thought of Patricia, half dressed and vulgar, coming out to greet these grieving families. How would I explain that? *Oh, I'm sorry. You see, I'm possessed by a victim who was murdered by a serial killer.* That was not what my clients came to me to hear.

So today, I looked myself in the mirror as I fixed my hair and face.

"I don't want a peep out of you. I want to be alone. You can't keep acting out." I turned from my reflection and looked around my empty bedroom. "Stay put and don't make a noise. I have to work." There was no response. Good.

I heard the knock on my outside office door and went to answer it gladly. Today was about life, not death. There was a woman who was wondering how to go about telling her family she wanted to get married. Oh, the trials and tribulations of the blossoming heart. I wished all the problems brought to me were this lovely.

I let this beautiful young woman in, and she gave me a big hug, filled with excitement and fear all rolled up together. My motherly instinct started to flow, and I guided her over to the couch and took her hand. She did not know

THE HAUNTING OF THE GEMINI   209

that her reading had already begun. The physical touch was like plugging an electrical cord into a socket. I was powered up. Her voice began to go in and out. Her eyes became an open pool. I looked deep inside her.

She started to get a bit lost, so I offered her water and a tissue for her tears. This relaxed her at least a little, and we continued. I often begin my sessions by sharing stories with my clients, using things only they would relate to or recognize. The young woman finally began to relax and had just cracked a smile when a loud noise from upstairs made her jump. *Crap.* I tried to laugh it off. "I'm sure it's just a ghost," I said.

Her eyes grew huge. "You have ghosts?" she murmured.

My dear, if only you knew.

The bumps and bangs got louder. "There's nothing to fear. I'm sure they're just saying hello," I said cheerfully. I excused myself as nonchalantly as I could and raced upstairs. There was no one there, nothing out of place. I returned to my office.

"My apologies," I said. "Let's get back to you."

The sweet thing asked if her intended really loved her. I could answer yes with certainty. I knew she would marry this man. I saw their child, yet to be born, sitting in her lap. Her life unfolded for me. There were a few future roadblocks that I made her aware of, but what's life if it doesn't make us stop and change lanes every now and then?

It was a session of pure happiness, and I think it helped my heart as much as hers. On her way out, she stopped and hugged me and then asked if I had a young child—a girl. I stared at her and stammered that I did not and that there was no little girl in this area. She shook her head. She said that when she had walked up to the house before her appointment, she saw a little girl sitting on the outside steps, holding on to the railing. I suggested that it might be the lighting playing tricks on her.

"No, Ms. Jackie," she insisted as she left. "I saw a little girl on the steps."

After she left, I locked up behind her, exhausted not from the session but from what she had seen on my stoop. I stomped upstairs. "Great . . . now you're showing yourselves to clients . . . just what I need . . ."

I was just getting warmed up—I can yell a blue streak, which shouldn't be surprising—when I smelled fresh coffee and stale cigarette smoke. That shut me up. I turned the corner into the kitchen and there, leaning over the counter, was Patricia. A pile of letters sat in front of her. They were all from the Zodiac Killer.

"I'm going to write him," she said, blowing smoke in my face. She grabbed a handful of letters and shoved them at me. "Look at these letters. Did you read them?" she asked me. "He's tricking you, Jackie. Just waiting to escape."

"Patricia, he already knows how to come in," I said. "First in spirit, then in body."

Patricia sucked on her cigarette. "You're seeing what didn't happen yet, Jackie. The escape of the New York City Zodiac Killer. You're seeing what he will do—what's to come. He's using your psychic energy to transport himself.

He's reliving his glory, the bodies lined up like trophies. And the letters are proof. What he did, and what will be."

I stood there in shock. She sounded just like me! Which one of us was real? Or were we both? God, my head hurt. I just wanted her to leave. I lunged for her, trying to scare her away. The letters fluttered to the floor, and behind them was only an empty room. There was no one but me, holding a half-finished cigarette. A cup of joe steamed on the counter, surrounded by spilled sugar and cream, as if the person fixing the coffee had rushed out.

I could taste the smoke in my mouth as I put out the cigarette. I rinsed my mouth at the sink and turned around. There were letters all over the floor. Pictures of Eddie. Drawings by Eddie. His signature with the symbol of the Gemini. "We are both. We are twins. We are each other."

He was using me to roam past those secure bars, past the armed guards and concrete walls, toward me. He was trying to take me over. *If I can't be out . . . I can be you; I can live in your eyes . . . Slowly I can gain the power and knowledge of the outside world so when the timing is right and all is lined up, the planetary signs will open the gate to hell and I shall roam, and drink once more.*

But his victim was interfering. Her smoke stayed in my nose as I began to gather the letters, matching them with the proper envelopes. It was as though I were seeing them for the first time. There among them was one bigger envelope with . . . *my God*. Him requesting information, needing research on how to get out of a maximum-security prison, on guns and weapons that could take out a small city. Asking me to assist him, step-by-step.

I thought I'd had all of his letters boxed away—all the pictures, the handprints, the mask. Where had these others been? Why didn't I remember seeing them? I sat there on my kitchen floor and read them. Letter after letter, many posted a year and a half ago, all telling me to keep them safe and to use a different name when writing back. It was as if the letters I knew about were meant for me, while these were for someone else, even though they were all addressed to Jackie.

I gathered them up and tied them with a leather strap that I found among them on the floor. Where had I been hiding them all this time? I went up to my bedroom and stood quietly, looking deep inside myself. Holding the bundle, I moved in front of the mirror and stared past my own image. The mirror began to move like water, and the little waves parted to reveal scenes . . . faces . . . a child and a woman holding hands and going into my closet. A deep walk-in, it had top-to-bottom shelves and cubbies that Will built for me years ago. Lots of places to hide things.

I turned from the mirror and went to my closet, pulling things down, rummaging through shelves and drawers. Finally, I found a drawer in the back that was empty except for a Polaroid picture. Of Eddie. He had written on it: *My friend Jackie Barrett*, and my sign, Sagittarius. Then came his name and the Gemini symbol. And a stick figure drawing of a child. This spot, where I hadn't looked for years, was where the letters were hidden. Why would the ghosts of a woman and a child hide all this? To save the world from what they endured at the hands of serial killers? Is it possible for the dead to save the living?

Yes, I thought as I sat on my closet floor with tears in my eyes. *Yes, it is possible.* They interact with us every day. They come to us in our dreams. They influence our decisions. They give us clues. We use the phrase, "I had a feeling . . ." They live alongside us. They love.

They exist.

Sometimes, when I talked to Eddie on the phone, he would answer my questions about his planning and his crimes.

"How does it feel, Jackie, asking me questions and knowing all the things I have done? Only we know . . . I can hear your voice change when we talk about the screams, the little animals, the women and men. It's inside of you now, too . . . Did you know when someone screams hard enough from the gut, the extreme panic yaks over and you foam from the mouth like a wild dog. Wild, right?"

Before Eddie found Patricia, his prized soul, he would walk dark alleys and stare into corners and windows, looking for the right victim. He would climb trees and look down on potential prey. The hunt was on. He told me he had done so many things, to so many people. Things the police didn't know about. They had no idea what he was capable of.

Like the evening he decided to lurk outside an apartment building. A man came out with a little dog on a leash. When the man turned to go back inside, he carefully aimed his gun and pulled the trigger. The door swung shut behind the man, but it was all glass, so he could watch the suffering as the man fell to the ground. He wasn't dead, but he was in pain, so Eddie had been at least somewhat successful. And the fear in the dog's face as his master collapsed was even better.

He watched carefully. He was curious to see how the man would struggle. And it was fascinating to see the loyal little dog sitting next to him, barking the whole time. He wanted to get close enough to watch his victim's eyes lose color and turn gray as he took his last breath, but it was not to be. He walked away, wanting more.

He began to practice his shooting. He would go sit near the highway by Highland Park and fire at passing cars. He shot at police vehicles a couple of times, always slinking off before he was discovered. He took target practice in bad neighborhoods littered with abandoned cars. The bullets on metal—ping, ping, ping—confirmed his aim. He set fire to a few of the clunkers, just because he felt like it.

He sauntered through Times Square several times and enjoyed asking the cops what time it was. Like he was an ordinary guy. He even asked them if they had any clues about the Zodiac Killer yet. That was particularly amusing.

And then he expanded his plans. He wanted to increase his body count tenfold. New York was full of places that were always packed with people. He spent the years after his Central Park shooting sizing up his city's landmarks. He considered Rockefeller Center, with its double bonus of office workers and tourists. He thought he could shatter the windows with a slingshot—that would be terrifying. He made a big one of solid wood and carved the Gemini sign into it. It could fling a six-pound rock. And then he was patient. He planned to wait until Christmas, when the whole place was packed with revelers, ice skaters using that famous rink, people gawking at the Christmas tree. Crowds of people made him smile, especially when they were running for their lives. But the flying rock would only be a diversion. He would plant pipe bombs in the lockers at the side of the ice rink—that would be the real show.

He thought about the Empire State Building. He rode to the top and looked out through one of the telescopes. The view was beautiful, and he saw in his mind's eye the change he could make if he bombed it—the smoke and the chaos, the fire trucks trying to get through the choked streets, the screaming victims. It made him feel young and powerful.

Neither of these plans ever came to fruition, thank God. But he made his own bombs, just like he made his own guns, using instructions from military books and catalogs. And he prowled the city looking for the best places to put his handiwork. The sewer system, the manholes, schools, the posts where cops stood. He walked the subway tunnels and noticed the homeless people who lived deep in their depths. He set a few fires there, hoping to burn someone, but never knew whether he actually had.

He set several bombs in the subway tunnels and listened to them go off as he stood back by the station turnstiles. He was pretty sure he hadn't successfully hurt anyone, but at least he got the terrified reactions he wanted. He carefully mapped out all sorts of other potential locations. If he could hit them all, his kill count would be up into the thousands. Nice stacks of body parts, everywhere.

When he needed a rest from his bombs and his maps, he would break into houses. Any little crack—an open window, an unlatched basement door—he would slip through and then just sit. Once, a family ate dinner upstairs while he lurked below and listened. He said he loved spying on people. He loved that they did not know how close the devil was.

One night in 1994, as he sank deeper and deeper into the devil's world, Eddie told me that he lay in bed in his little room, yelling and hitting himself, but the beast would not leave. And then he heard laughter. It was his laugh, and he turned to see himself sitting at the small school desk near the bed.

"Get up, you coward, and listen to me. You welcomed me and I heard you. You asked me to guide you and I did." He was no longer laughing. "You asked me to protect you from those pigs, those cops, and I did. You got caught, you fool with a gun. And what did I do? Did I run and leave you? Did I run under your mother's skirt? No! I made sure your fingerprints didn't show up when they threw you in jail. I made sure your gun didn't work. They held you the whole day in lockup. You telling me, 'That's it, I'm caught.'

"I got you out . . . the Zodiac lives. They opened that cell and you walked out free, thanks to Lucifer, your angel. And they gave you back the gun that worked the minute you walked out of that jail.

"Just think . . . I helped you become the dark sky over the city of New York. And you forsake me now? Stand up! Put that mask on and look through that mirror—not in it, but through it! Look at your army of souls.

"I own you. We shall always be together. My flesh is yours."

Eddie got out of bed, stood in front of the mirror, and became the devil's son. Eddie was so small now that he—this powerful force in front of the mirror—could put him in his pocket. So he did. And he went forth again. And he never looked back. His next victim, he remembered, was a pathetic homeless man in an abandoned car. He set it on fire. He loved fire; it left nothing behind. He had done that man a favor, too.

He took joy, I think, in letting me know all of his secrets.

"I used to go into the confession booth in church to throw up on the priest," he laughed. "Father, I have sinned! I'd throw all those bodies up right on his back, like a big blood cross, yeah, let him carry it around. I left, feeling the hunger again and again.

"It's easy telling you. Seems like you knew by looking

inside of me. Or just maybe me being in you! How many times have you run into the devil, Jackie? How many times can you get away?"

I tried to distance myself, knowing that he was looking for that crack, that weakness we all have—at least those of us with a conscience. Because, of course, he didn't have one himself.

"Did you ever see someone trapped in a car blazing up, banging on the windows, trying to escape? People not so far away in their own world, high on drugs, playing music, taking a shit. It was an everyday thing in Highland Park. Come on, not one person knew what I looked like. I sat right alongside all those people."

I knew that. He walked where he chose, and no one remembered him. Why didn't he get caught? He laughed at my question like a shy little boy. "I was doing those pigs a favor. Cleaning up the streets for them. They would immediately blame it on drug wars . . . That park was a nest for any drug you wanted and the filth that came along with it. Whores, pimps, pushers, addicts that would blow you for a quarter or less. I remember looking to sit on a bench—waiting for a fresh piece of meat—and was I fucking hungry. You have to watch where you sit. Damn cum on the bench. Some people have no pride. Probably some junkie getting someone off for some loose change. Piss and shit all over. And you think those cops want to come into that world and get their hands dirty?"

When the police first saw Patricia's body slumped against a fence, they thought it was another overdose, he said, laughing. "How the fuck could you think that?"

He talked about several of his crimes during our conversation.

"And the man walking his dog, Jackie, I shot him not to kill him but to watch him squirm, beg for help . . . Down he went in his own liquid life, that red, thick fluid that keeps us alive. I did that around 1992. That was just a quickie. You know, a fast fix. If you compare it to sex— because it felt so good—that was only measured . . . like a blow job . . . It was a tease to my bloodlust. I didn't even bother to see if it made the papers. More happens than most know. Do you think everything was reported? Plus, the pigs don't want to let everything out. They have to save something that only the perpetrator would know—like taking a body part."

I shuddered. "Did you ever take a body part?" I asked.

"No—I take the whole body and soul. I'm a true collector. Now, some who kill only women may take the panties or snip a nipple off, just one . . . but I'm not prejudiced. Everyone is game. When a wild animal hunts, it doesn't say, 'I can only kill a deer.' Anything that moves is hunted.

"I traveled around the city a lot. Watching people, the daily routines, even what they wore on what days. Who goes to lunch on certain days in certain restaurants. When the cops took breaks. I knew when certain people got paid. Watching the girls spend their checks on makeup and silk stockings. I thought about those silky stockings going all the way up those legs. I would love to split her—all of them—in half, like gutting a cow. Just had a thought—wouldn't that make an identical twin? Two halves make a whole, right?"

He went on.

"Jackie . . . where do all the people go when they are missing? Where are they?"

"They die, Eddie," I said.

"Very good," he replied. "If you have a mark, you'll only get blamed for the mark. Like the Boston Strangler, I'm sure there were other victims but they couldn't prove it. If you break into a woman's home and kill by strangulation . . . but what about if you kill on the street by a gunshot? Oh, that must be a different predator. You're right, Jackie, I am a lethal weapon. I never stopped killing. Just because I didn't leave a letter . . . The pipe bombs I tested in the subway worked [but] I didn't leave a letter on the platform. Don't you see, I come from all directions at any time. That's the frightening part. You will never know where I am. But for you, Jackie, just look under your bed."

How many people do you need to take down a city, he asked me. Only one, he said. And how many task forces do you need to find him? A lot, because it would take a big group of highly intelligent people to find that one man. Why? Because cops aren't born to kill. They're trained. "Makes a big difference. Just like you, Jackie. How many people could do what you do or see what you see? We can be twins. I'll give you the clues, and you try to stop me."

EIGHTEEN

——◆——

Another birthday. Will and Joanne always went all out on my special day, and they didn't disappoint this year. Will woke me with flowers and breakfast in bed. I sat up carefully as he came in, keeping the covers over me. I knew my nightly prowl would show on my aching feet. Most mornings they were covered in dry blood and caked dirt. It wasn't my dirt or blood, it was Patricia's, and for each mile I walked on her feet, I did feel that I was closer to understanding. My nocturnal travels certainly hadn't gone unnoticed by my husband, but today I didn't want to show off the evidence and ruin whatever he had planned for the day.

As I pulled myself up in bed, something knocked against my hand. I peeked under the covers and the smell of booze hit me. An empty fifth of whiskey lay against my side. I had no memory of getting it, or drinking it. I don't drink, never have. The intoxicating liquid that quieted Patricia's restless mind would only stir mine like a pot of boiling gumbo.

I slid the bottle under my pillow when Will wasn't looking and sniffed my own breath. Nothing. I sighed in relief. I hadn't had any whiskey. But still, I couldn't let Will see this. I took the tray of food in order to mask my anxiety. How would I hide all of this?

"Can't a girl get a shower?" I said, shooing him out.

"You win," he laughed. "But hurry, we have a whole day planned."

As soon as the door closed behind him, I threw back the covers. Pillows went flying as I searched for any other souvenirs of my night. There was nothing else in the bed. Slowly, I knelt down to look underneath. I felt silly, like a kid checking for the monster under the bed after mommy says good night. I pulled up the bed skirt, and the silliness evaporated in a cloud of horror.

A woman lay flat on her back, with her arms crossed upon her chest. Her face was deathly pale. She was wearing my clothes. I gagged at the smell of the decomposing body and clamped my hand over my mouth. I could not comprehend how she had gotten there. At times like this, it is virtually impossible to hold a thought in one's head. I sure couldn't. My brain just froze. I don't know how long I crouched there, staring at this corpse in my clothes.

And then she burst out laughing.

"I got you that time, Jackie. You should have seen your face!"

Anger melted my frozen brain. I reached under the bed and grabbed at Patricia.

"Come on, get out! Get my goddamn clothes off. I'm going to call the cops!"

"Go ahead," she cackled. "They'll think you're crazy and put you away. They can't see me!"

She rolled out from under the bed, talking about how the two of us liked to hang out with her friends in the park at night. I mingled well, she told me, as she sat down on the bed and started in on my breakfast, moving food around my plate.

"Jackie, come here. This is good shit. Look, you have a silver spoon, isn't that sweet? And crispy bacon."

I sank down on the bed, put my head in my hands, and begged her to get out of my life.

"I'm not in your life," she yelled at me. "You're me, Jackie. You gave me life back! I have Will, too. Soon I will be whole again, alive."

"What do you want? Just tell me," I pleaded. If I helped her, I suddenly thought, maybe I could save myself. I had started out wanting to do just that—solve whatever problem she had—but these horrible months with her had made me so angry. I hated her. But if I could tamp down my rage and get her cooperation, maybe I could save her, and she would go away. Then I would be saving myself, too.

"It's not that easy," she said. She finally sat still and a tear fell, hitting the bed. "I was lost, and you found me."

"You can't stay," I said.

She stood and started to cry as she walked backward into a corner of the bedroom. She kept going and just faded away. I was left sitting on my bed with bacon scattered all over and her sobs ringing in my ears.

I picked up the mess that was my birthday breakfast, shoved the empty liquor bottle into my purse, and dragged myself to the shower. All I wanted was to wash off all the dirt. I had absolutely no memory of what had taken place the night before. God knows what I had done.

I was in there so long, the bathroom filled with steam. I got out, wrapped myself in a towel, and was about to wipe off the mirror when someone grabbed me from behind. One arm wound around my waist and the other hand wrapped around my throat. I saw black gloves through the steam. His nose and mouth pressed against the back of my neck, and he sniffed me like an animal would.

"Jackie . . . it's your birthday." The tall man in black began to sing very slowly. "Happy Birthday to you . . . Happy birthday to you . . . Happy birthday dear Jane . . . oops . . . Jackie . . . I mean Patricia . . ."

He giggled and then bit down on my ear.

"This is your life," he said through clenched teeth. "Feel me. Breathe me. As long as she stays, I follow. I am your dark, depraved secret. You will answer my calls. You will feed me the knowledge I request."

I closed my eyes. Over and over in my head, I pleaded with myself to wake up. *He can't hurt me; he's in prison; he can't hurt me.* He went still, as if he could hear my thoughts. His voice changed from the giggly to the demonic.

"You want to kill, like me," he rumbled. "You want revenge. That poor little girl, that sweet little girl. How easy it was, like taking candy from a baby.

"And that other one. Ha! You know, if you didn't let

her in, the world would have never remembered her. The insane asylum misses her. But we can fix that. You will take her place. Oh, that white jacket with those really awesome leather restraints would look so sexy on you." He rubbed against me. "How cozy we can be."

His grip tightened. The sound of squeaky wheels filled the bathroom.

"We all have desires, Jackie," the tall man in black said. "You know, your ghostly friend that jumps in and out of you, yeah, that party girl—she took a liking to Will. Oh, your big savior, your protector! I heard he got all lovely with her. You going to let him get away with that? Fucking around on you with a dead woman?"

The rusty wheels got closer. Louder. I turned to see, and I was alone in the bathroom. He was gone, but I knew that his grip on me remained.

A knock on the door startled me.

"Mom?"

I let Joanne in, and she wished me happy birthday with a big hug. The right kind of hug. She pulled away and looked at me. "What's wrong? You okay?"

I just had to ask her. "What happened last night? Was I out? Was I home before Will got in?"

She was puzzled, I could tell.

"What? You and Will were downstairs in the lounge."

She said she had gotten home from her date at midnight, and we were downstairs playing Christmas music and laughing like teenagers.

"It was good to just hear you two having fun. It's been a long time."

But it wasn't me.

"Lock the door and sit down," I said as her worried look grew worse. "It's that woman. I can't shake her. Most of the time, I'm not me."

Joanne protested. "You had a party last night. You and Will. I heard it!"

Knowing that words wouldn't explain it, I grabbed her hand and took her downstairs—to see what had happened at this "party." The Christmas tree was out. Glitter and ornament balls were all over. Tinsel had been flung all over my cherished artwork. Someone had taken a lot of glee in "decorating." But it hadn't been me. I always procrastinated for as long as I could every year, because getting out the decorations meant going into the garage and digging past all the other things I had in storage down there—like all of the things Eddie had sent me, and a bunch of other boxes, full of letters from other serial killers who've written me. But this year, someone had obviously done it for me in late November, and they had done a spectacularly bad job.

"What a freaking mess! I did this? No way. This isn't me! Look at this mess!" I do not do messes. This had to be fixed. Right then.

"Jo, can you please tell Will to give me an hour? I have to clean this up."

"Let me help you," she smiled. She ran to the intercom and told Will that we were doing "girl stuff" and would be done soon. My husband, no fool on that score, got the message and stayed away.

As we picked everything up, I asked her if she had been seeing anything strange.

"Us? You've got to be kidding," she said. She had a point. Everything about us was strange. "Our lives are haunted!" she said. "As in, no matter where we go or how far or fast we run—it's there before we are. I used to think when I was young that it was our home. Every home we had—from fancy doorman buildings, to big old houses, to new ones just built."

She had seen some things, that was for sure.

"Mom," she said. "We'll get through this."

I did not share her certainty.

"Joanne, promise me one thing . . . don't let me go."

Now she looked frightened. She grabbed my hand like a small child would.

"Never, Mom . . . never . . ."

I would try to quiet the battle in my head by writing things down.

> *I have an enemy who lives in my head.*
> *She crawls at night into my bed.*
> *She holds me tight, clinging to a thread.*
> *Enemy, enemy, yes, you are dead.*
> *Enemy, enemy who now lives inside,*
> *After all of this, I have not a place to hide.*
> *You came to see the world through me*
> *After his killing spree.*
> *Fragments of my life sprinkled around,*
> *As you fell hard to the ground.*
> *The party ended,*

The lights turned down,
The killing man still walks around.

But even my poetry would get taken over by Patricia.

I see no fortune or fame,
Only a hundred holes, and he is to blame.
My name is Patricia, and I am alive.
In you I shall reside.
No one will know, no one could see,
With you, we can be all three.
Little girl, little girl, don't come in.
Run, run, while I'll eat my sin.
Enemy I am not . . .
Just a girl the world forgot.

At this rate, a mental institution was not far off for me, I knew. Either I had to put Patricia back where she belonged, or both of us were going to end up in a straitjacket.

The caller ID said Great Meadow again.

He'd had to lay low in between the shootings, Eddie explained. That was when he made his own map of the city, dotted with targets. And what if he had succeeded with his bombs?

"I would have laid low for another few years. Maybe a nice town, one of those quiet little country towns where door locks don't exist. Maybe work in a church. Clean-cut, no tattoos, no ponytails. Just a nice guy everyone wants to meet. I told you, Jackie, right under the nose. Now, that's the greatest trick. Just don't stand out."

But that is not what happened. Eddie made himself very noticeable, and he got caught. "What happened that day?" I asked.

That day in 1996, his bedroom was full of bombs and guns, Eddie told me, because the next day, he planned on taking down the city. He was trying to prepare, but his sister and her boyfriend were in the apartment. Music was playing loudly, and he couldn't think straight. For the first time since this had all begun, he was getting nervous. His sister making all that noise was fucking him up. A rage came over him, and a voice yelled in his head. "Kill her and that boyfriend now."

He started to bang his head against the wall. He didn't want to. He yelled, "No!" and the map—the routes to all of his bombing locations—caught fire, even though there were no lit candles or open flames in the room. He did shoot his sister, but his deal fell apart anyway. The devil turned him in.

"Why couldn't anyone describe you or identify you?" I asked.

"You're not listening to me. The devil has his way of making you see what he wants. Let's face it, if he didn't, I would have been caught a long time ago. Remember, I'm just a low-grade killer, right?"

I asked him what he meant by that.

"Who am I? I had no money. No education. No food.

I lived in the projects. No father. No fancy clothes. Nothing but everything. Unstoppable. The day I signed that paper [with] the mark of the Zodiac, it was something out of this world. Like I had a twin. One body, two people." He went on about the devil helping him to appear differently. "I was face-to-face with many. They still couldn't remember. They thought it was a black man because that's what people saw . . . I left notes in the beginning, giving them clues. I was opening the gates in the sky. Putting spells on those notes. Nothing is what it seems. Then my lust for blood was so strong, I was thinking about drinking it, too, [but] I didn't care for the flavor of the weak bastards."

For the second series of shootings, he had the notes but didn't leave them, he said. "Why should I give them any more clues? I knew everyone's sign. There are no coincidences. He gave me the power of sight, confusion, and terror. The list goes on, Jackie."

"But why add to the list, Eddie, once you were caught?" I pushed him. "Why confess to shooting somebody in June 1994, months after the police thought you had stopped?"

"I confessed to the June killing. They haven't found the bodies. They just didn't connect it to me. They messed up big time. I had nothing to lie about; why should I? I'm a killer, a natural-born killer. I live to kill."

As for Patricia, the stabbing didn't fit his pattern—they never would have charged him with that one. So why did he confess to it? I asked.

"I confessed to killing Patricia because she is mine. That's my work of art. It takes a lot to carve someone up. I was proud of my work. There was more, but the bodies went to the city dump, the morgue. No one looked. No one cared.

"I cared enough to collect them all. The faces, the space they took up. They live inside of me now. You may have gotten Patricia out, but you'll have a lot more work, because I have killed many."

My battles with Patricia continued. But the more I fought, the more I resisted, the more she'd take over. More nightly travels. More mysterious stains on my feet. More remnants of parties I didn't remember.

Sometimes I actually found myself feeling jealous of her free spirit. That tilted halo and the hands holding a smoke and a bottle. Life was short, baby. Live it up. She had fun where I couldn't. Like with the Christmas decorations. She had made time for Will and had had a great evening. I could barely manage a smile nowadays.

That was another sign that I was slipping further away. I would stare into the mirror and feel my face, trying to hold on to any little detail that would trigger my memory—Jackie's memory—of who I was. My name would sound so unfamiliar. My body would go cold. If I stood still long enough, I would become stiff. The breath would leave my body in little puffs of air that would frost my lips. The thought of death was always there.

NINETEEN

In the decade and a half that Eddie Seda has been in prison, you'd think people would have forgotten about him, especially people with no connection to the crimes, no connection to him before he was caught, no connection even to New York. But that is not the case. He gets letters, all the time, from all over the world. Most of them are from women, and they all want him to write back. They all want to get to know the "real" Heriberto. They all want to know his "side of the story."

One chatty letter-writer said, "Dear Heriberto. . . I am writting [sic] to you for no reason other than to become your Pen Pal/Friend." She asked if he had hobbies, if he'd had friends growing up, what he used to do for fun. "I have enclosed my photograph that way you have an idea whom your [sic] writing [sic] with and I'll send more. I <u>really</u> hope you reply and we can become pen pals." A different letter stated, "I'm a very genuine person and through future correspondence I hope you'll see that for yourself . . . I'm here to listen to whatever you want to tell me and answer any questions you may have for me; I'm very open-minded and always listen with an open heart."

"I've always been very fascinated in crime and what makes people do the unimaginable," another letter stated. "Personnally [*sic*] I feel that not many people have taken the time to get to know you on a personal level or see you as the person you are not what your [*sic*] convicted of." This one at least had the sense to put a post-office box as her return address.

Another one quite cheerfully stated that the author had been corresponding with prison inmates for more than two years and gave him her street address. Ladies, I would not recommend doing this. I asked Eddie once what he would do if he was out of prison and approached by someone like that who wanted to "get to know" him. He told me he'd probably kill her. That went for any of his fans.

The other type of mail that Eddie received came from people looking for a clinical relationship with him, not a personal one—researchers doing studies and surveys about prisoners and so forth. Most of these requests kept to the theme of educating the public. One psychologist sent him a fourteen-page questionnaire that included questions that asked for yes/no or some-times/always/never responses, ones that required him to rate on a scale of 1 to 7, and a few that would need a written response that shouldn't take more than a paragraph to answer. Though I wholeheartedly agree that the public needs to know how people like Eddie think, sending out a mass questionnaire to serial killers is not helpful. They're just going to bullshit you. Plus, the mind of each one of these serial killers is very different. You can't lump them all together with a series of multiple-choice questions. Each killer is a whole different species.

Eddie does not respond to researchers. But he certainly offered me insight into his attitudes when he forwarded one of these letters on to me. "Just for jokes, Jackie, read this," he wrote in the top margin of the letter. Underneath that, he continued, "Speaking of jokes, your [*sic*] turning into my kill. Did you go to the park yet?" His handwriting continued down the sides of the page. "That night oh the signs are all in place now. Don't you hate when you feel all the stabbing sharp pains? I can make it better. How many times must you die?" And at the bottom: "And this is the Zodiac speaking again."

As for the letter, Eddie said, "I used [it] to wipe my ass with."

Even *America's Most Wanted* approached Eddie, asking him to help them "get a better understanding of what causes some individuals to repeatedly act violently . . . By doing this interview, we think you'll give our national audience a clearer perception of you, your situation, your actions, and why you did what you did."

At the top of that letter, which Eddie also forwarded to me, he wrote:

Jackie, They think they know me, HA HA HA which one—

Eddie called.

"It's time to take notes, Jackie. Who am I to you? Who am I to the world?"

I started to speak.

"No," he said, "don't interrupt me. I showed you things only others can imagine. Yes, I do exist! You can lock me up tight with chains, shackles, thick bars, and barbed wire. Tell me when to sleep and wake. Give me rancid food. And guess what? It doesn't affect me. I live in this world, as imperfect as I am. By eye, one can't tell. By actions, I brought people closer to God. Oh, God save me as I plunge the knife in your chest, and only then will the devil get his credit. Only then will the word *evil*, pure evil, be printed across every headline. The Zodiac strikes again! And yes, again!

"Believe, Jackie . . . believe in me. I am one of the many that have been set out into the world by the blood of the devil. I blow in the winter wind, bloom with the spring flowers, set beautiful sunsets. I move through the parks of laughing children and sit in the dark, curtains drawn."

He was enjoying himself. "I laugh at the public thinking I did what I did out of frustration. Psychiatrists trying to diagnose me—first you must go to hell. Then priests fearing me. Oh, they knew they weren't authorized to cast the devil out. The collar didn't make them strong. Their faith was weak."

I stopped trying to break into his barrage of words.

"When you're walking and feel the crowd thin . . . You pick up your pace, looking behind, hoping it was just your imagination . . . It was I! It was easy. Even the police didn't want to believe." He cackled. "My notes to them were just a prank. Child's play. That's right. Ignore what's in your face—the shootings, the letters . . . someone just whacking off on those pigs. I was right in their face at all times. My master protected me, controlling the situation.

"How can we convince the public of such dark forces if the police and homicide detectives didn't want to open their eyes to my existence? Why didn't they listen to my coming, my warning, all my notes? It's fear of the truth.

"I will tell you why. I only am seen when it is convenient. When those holy people run to church at times of need, repenting their own sins to feel better. Only then will the word *devil* pass their lips . . ."

He was on a roll, talking faster and faster.

"I lay on my cement slab of a bed, looking up at the cement-and-cinder-block ceiling, all snug like a slimy slug—oops, I mean bug. Ha. Just thinking how many children all over the world are in bed. The lights go out, you hold your little fingers around the blanket, pulling it up easy, ever so easy . . . knowing that monster under the bed lives.

"You're alone now, sweat coming down your face.

Your eyes squeeze tight. You open them just a crack, waiting to witness what every child knows—the good and evil. You feel me. You smell me. You see a little shadow on the wall. You scream. Mommy! Daddy! Your parents run in, turning on the light, coming to your aid. Your big, brave dad, who every kid thinks is his hero, says, 'It's okay, I'm here now.'"

He switched focus for a moment. "For me, I never met my father, nor do I care. I never even asked what his name was. Even as a child, it didn't matter to me. I had a mission—yes, I shall grow to collect the souls and wear my mask well."

Then it was back to those childhood fears that everyone had, except him.

"He looks under your bed just to ease your little mind. 'See, nothing at all!' He checks the closet, moving things around. He should have looked over his shoulder. Your mother holds you tight, comforting you. All along, you know the truth! You believe! You're put back to bed with a kiss. That's the thing I count on! That's right . . ."

I was listening to one of the most evil creatures of our time. He pulled out that powerful book and scratched his name in it. He wrote a chapter in hell, and I don't know if it's finished.

When I was eight years old, my dad and I took the family station wagon to town to run some errands. That car always seemed huge to me . . . until he got in it. Once my father fit his giant body inside, it became compact, like a circus car, his head almost touching the top. I held back a laugh when I saw him crouching behind the wheel. He turned to smile at me as I sat on the seat with my knees up against my chest, and my rope belt caught his eye. It was part of my standard uniform, which included scuffed jeans and T-shirts. I was more tomboy than not, and he always let me be.

His eyes met mine, and I could read his thoughts right then as easily as if they were printed on paper. *Someday, she'll need that rope.* I thought back. *Yes, Dad, I know I will.* He grabbed my hand and spoke aloud: "Never let go, Jackie. Do you understand? Remember the things you'll someday need."

I thought that over as we continued toward town. We passed the swamp, and the children who were always there waved at me as we drove by. I never waved back because I knew they were dead, and I wasn't quite sure how my father would react to my acknowledging dead people. That was why I sat with my legs up on the seat—so I could hide my head between my knees when the ghosts came around. But having to ride past the swamp was worth it if I got to hang out with my dad. Going to the supermarket with him was always an adventure, and most of the time it even got me a piece of Bazooka bubble gum. I loved those big pink bricks and their wrappers with the comics inside.

I was thinking about that treat when I got out of the car in the hot parking lot. I walked around to the driver's side of the car and stopped at the expression on my dad's face. Then I followed his gaze. He was staring at the poor box.

That's what we called it, anyway. It was the huge, dark-green metal collection box for the Salvation Army, and it sat in the supermarket parking lot. It was about six feet tall and four feet wide, and today, it was making noises. I walked slowly toward it, looking back and forth from it to my dad. I heard movement and rustling coming from inside it. From the look on his face, I knew he had, too.

"Come on," he said, waving me on. "Just walk past it, Jacks."

Whatever was inside the box seemed to hear my foot-steps. I could sense its awareness that I was coming near. *Don't talk . . . She's coming closer . . . She could hear us . . .* I wanted desperately to get out of there.

My dad bent down to my eye level. "Look at me, and just walk. Don't run. Never run."

The box, solid metal, began to move from side to side. Then all the voices in it spoke at once—millions of them, chattering and whispering. I leaped into the arms of my best protector and buried my head in his shoulder, hoping he would whisk me off to safety in the store. Instead, he sat me down on the hood of the station wagon and unhooked my gripping hands from his shirt.

"You will learn," he said, "when you run past the fear, it has won. When you run, it runs faster. When you hide, it only lets you think you got away."

His words sank in, leaving an impression that would last me a lifetime. I stared over his shoulder at the box and closed my eyes. My mind went inside, through the many layers of clothing, to look for the bodies that went with the voices. But all I found were the residues left behind on the belongings of others. The fragments of their lives. I opened my eyes and looked at my father.

I knew I had no place to hide.

I was on my way into Manhattan, off to catch the express bus a few blocks from my house. I tried to ignore the noise around me. So many people bustling by, with so many thoughts and disappointments I tried so hard not to hear. I was attempting to tune it all out when I turned the corner and saw it. The poor box. Sitting in the middle of a city block in Brooklyn. I stopped short and stared. It was the same—same dark-green paint, same iron handle and mailbox-type slot for sliding in the donations. The sticker on the side was half-torn and scratched. It read only "Salvation"—the "Army" was missing.

I was getting jostled and pushed by pedestrians trying to get around me. No one seemed to notice the box. I walked forward, stopped in front of it, and put my ear against the side. Like that last time, so long ago, I could hear movements and voices. I closed my eyes, trying to separate the noises of the passersby around me from those inside the container. Everything slowed to a halt, and the air around me changed. It felt like an invisible bed sheet twisting and twirling around me, sharp snaps like a whip slapping my face.

Then I heard a growl, and the sound of something crawling up the inside of the box. The handle began to move, and the slot opened wide enough for me to see eyes looking out at me and hear a little girl's voice. She pleaded for help and started crying softly, but she didn't move. A small back corner of my brain said that she couldn't be real—for example, any real child stuck in this kind of prison would be hysterical and screaming. I looked around. No one even glanced at me as they walked by, and certainly no one stopped and offered to help. I turned back. Screw it. It was obvious that this was meant for me. I opened the slot wider and stuck my arm in, trying to grab the girl.

I twisted my body sideways and stretched farther into the box. A sharp yank on my arm pulled me forward. The side of my head slammed into the metal.

"Oh, Jackie," I heard his voice say. "You fell for it again. It's that easy. Right into my trap." He held my arm against the sharp edge of the donation slot. The pain ran through my body, and I thought I might faint. "How many times must you die before you learn?"

I turned my head as well as I could and looked into the slot. I saw the tall man in black, wearing a mask and sitting on a pile of clothes. His dark eyes burned into me.

"Oh God, help me," I whispered to myself.

He went still. "God? Who is God? A martyr on the Cross? A man that is worshipped without a belief of the Spirit? Do you believe, Jackie? When you see all the destruction, you know who I am . . ."

I stopped him with a voice that came from somewhere deep inside of me like a blast of thunder. "Yes! I do. I believe. I know God has walked beside me, held my hand."

My arm was suddenly released. Off balance, I fell back and into people passing on the street. I sat down on the pavement, trying to collect myself. My arm felt like it had been ripped out of its socket. People brushed past me without even stopping to look. And when one woman did, I heard her mutter something about needing to clean up the streets. I was less than human to her. Was I being shown how easy it was to be tossed away by society? Was this how Patricia had felt? Had she evoked disgust and revulsion, too? Even though she was just a person, frightened and alone?

A shadow came over me, and the smell of garbage filled the air. A hand came out of the darkness and the shape of him followed. "Take my hand, Jackie," said the tall man in black. "Your quest for humanity will be thrown aside, just like you are now. Did anyone help you? I am here, Jackie. I always was . . . God moved too slowly today . . . Take my hand . . ."

I sat, frozen with despair. His hand moved closer.

And then, a little girl walking by pointed right at me. "Mommy, look. A lady is crying on the ground." The child continued to point. "And there's a man with a mask on!"

The mother tried to tug her child away. "I don't see a man. Just a woman . . . She'll be okay," she said. The girl shook her off and ran toward me. The masked man turned and disappeared into the crowd. "Are you okay, lady?" her tiny voice asked.

I stood and tried to act normal, smiling at the apprehensive mother, who plainly wanted to get her kid away from me. But that one, that particular child, will someday understand what I have been fighting. Today, though she did not know it, she did the fighting for me.

God does exist.

TWENTY

———

I went to Highland Park, and I stood at that place where Patricia lay down to die so many years ago on that hot, steamy night. Eddie had talked about this place during our phone conversations and I'd listened, knowing that I would have to face it myself eventually. He called it the playground of the dead, and he told me he would pass among the drug addicts and the prostitutes, sizing them up carefully for their suitability as victims.

"It's been a long time," he said on the phone, talking to me as though I were Patricia. "Why haven't you gone back to that park?"

I knew now that Patricia wanted me to see what he had done. She wanted someone to help her. She wanted desperately to be loved. She wanted to feel normal, to leave behind the schizophrenia that had gripped her in life. And she didn't want to die alone, left behind like trash.

And so I finally got up the courage, and I went. I sat on the bench next to her and held her hand. We would relive her death in my vision. I saw him waiting for us, standing silently with a grin. His eyes I will never forget. Patricia and I looked at each other. It was time. We began our doomed walk, slowly up the steps in Highland Park.

I began to fade. Her body became solid, and I was the ghostly figure. I was the observer now, the medium going back in time to bring light when darkness falls. I held on to her hand. *Don't look at him.* She nodded, telling me that she could do this. We got to the top of the stairs, where she had been shot twice and stabbed more than one hundred times even while fighting back with everything she had. He was waiting.

"It's time to stop running from him," I said.

She took both of my hands in hers. "I'm ready." She laid herself down on the ground, on the spot countless people had walked over in the years since her temporal death. I went down on my knees next to her, and my tears began to flow.

"You are no longer lost, nor are you blind. My sweet love, my companion. No danger. No darkness. Accept the Kingdom and go home. No pain, no fear. You are in God's arms, traveling home . . . home . . ."

I bent to kiss her hands, still clutched in my own. She whispered in my ear. "I'm scared. I can't see. The sky is so close . . ."

"No, Patricia," I said, "you can always see."

My ghostly form held her and began to hum an old

Gospel song. As I rocked her, I thought that this child of God was all of us—you, me, our children. We all know her, somehow.

"Do you feel the sun?" I asked. "Do you see all the faces waiting for you? Let go, Patricia, and feel the eternity. Look past the stars."

"Don't let go, Jackie. I don't want to die alone. Not this way."

"I'm here," I whispered. "You're not alone. You're safe." I was crying on her shoulder as she hung on to what she thought was life all this time. Death was coming. *Dear Lord, take this soul and keep her close. Walk with her. Free her. Take her pain. Time is no more on this earth, and yours shall be the glory.*

I saw her lift off with a golden glow. Not even the Zodiac Killer could destroy such a spirit. As I watched her go, I remembered the old jazz funerals in New Orleans and could hear the trumpets playing "Just a Closer Walk with Thee."

> *When my feeble life is o'er,*
> *Time for me will be no more;*
> *Guide me gently, safely o'er*
> *To Thy kingdom shore, to Thy shore.*

We should all look to the heavens for our everlasting home, reunited with the ones we long for and welcomed with unconditional love.

I was left alone, kneeling on the spot where she had

died, twice. There was no trace of blood. It had been washed from her soul. And I was solid and whole once again. I pulled myself up and looked toward the sky. Good-bye, my friend.

One night soon after, I decided to retrace my steps. It had been almost three years since Patricia had first come to me, and I finally felt so at peace that I knew that kind of walk would not send me back down into the devilish tug-of-war I had endured for so long. At Bellevue, I stood and stared up. This time, the wind blew the torn curtain outward, as though it were pushing me away from that place. "Go . . . Jackie . . ." The words floated down to my ears, and I turned away with a smile.

I paused to wipe my nose, runny from the December chill, and saw a newspaper blowing in the gusty wind just a few feet away from me. My breath caught—not again—but I made myself grab the paper and look. The date was current, and there was no news of death. I let it go with another smile. It blew away slowly and came to rest against the door of the New York City medical examiner's office. I walked on.

My feet carried me toward Midtown, and I found myself in front of Macy's, the grand master of Christmas spectacle. The windows twinkled with lights, and bold, beautiful letters spelled out the store's holiday theme: "Believe." That, for me, had been easier said than done. But now, I took it as a sign from God, and I did believe.

I walked the length of the window displays until I came

to one with little Virginia's letter. Was there a Santa Claus? I looked at the display with wondering eyes. A little hand took mine, and I saw my Forever Guardian reflected in the glass. For that split second, she didn't have the wisdom and strength that I always relied on. She was just a child full of wonder and innocence—something neither one of us ever got to be in real life.

A car horn sounded on the street behind me. The little hand slid out of mine and disappeared as I turned around.

"Well," he said, puffing on a stinky little cigar as he leaned against a yellow cab, "it took you long enough."

"Tony!" I yelled in astonishment. "What brings you out?" I opened my arms wide. He felt like a long-lost friend.

"Look at ya! You'll catch your death out here in this cold. Get in!" He reached over and opened the car door. I looked one last time at all the lights that spelled "Believe" and then back at him. "That's some message," he said. Yeah, it sure was.

I got in the cab and buckled up. Our eyes met in the rearview mirror. "What about you? Don't you wear a seat belt?" I asked.

"Nah," he said, pulling away from the curb. "Don't need one anymore."

We both knew what that meant.

Tony turned his taxi toward the highway and the bridge. "So, did you learn something, Jackie?"

"Yeah, I did, Tony," I answered. "I know the answer to many things now."

We smiled at each other. He reached for the radio and asked if I liked music.

"Are you kidding? I grew up playing any instrument I could get my hands on," I laughed.

He grinned and turned on the radio. Frank Sinatra's voice filled the car. We started to sing along.

You're running high in April, shot down in May . . .

"Yeah, Jackie, I was shot down," Tony said.

That's life . . . That's life . . .

He delivered me home safely that night, and it was the last time I saw him. But I'm sure he still cruises the empty streets of Manhattan, the guardian of the roads. I believe.

Yes, Virginia, there is a Santa Claus.

Yes, Patricia, you are loved for you.

There was a time, when I was in the middle of everything—when I didn't know what Patricia wanted, only that she was schizophrenic and driving me down the same road—I would have peeled back my skin and bled out just to be rid of her. She took me to hell. But then she brought me back.

Even after Patricia passed on, I still walked through the streets at night. The empty sidewalks brought me an odd sense of peace. Do you ever say, "I wish I didn't have so much laid on me. Why is my life so hard? Why? Why? Why?" I did. But I don't now. After Patricia had gone, I found myself longing for her reckless smile. I walked alone and looked in shop windows, hoping to see her reflection just once more. But I didn't. Every once in a while, when I saw someone pushing through a crowd, it caught my attention—could it be Patricia? But then the person would turn and make eye contact, and it wasn't her. She had passed on to a place where she no longer needed me. Her soul was free, finally, from her killer's grasp. And my soul was slowly becoming my own again as well.

She wasn't able to give herself as much as she ended up giving me. She forced me to look in my own mirror—the hardest thing a person can do. I know now that I also was murdered in a former life, and that I still have work to do to find the peace that Patricia now has. I now tell her, "Go! Don't ever come back. Freedom in death is just as important as in life. It's yours now." Eddie can no longer hold her.

I kept the journal that I wrote when I was possessed by her. It has her words in it, and I often reread them. They are the pages of a pained mind and soul. But then there is the last entry. It is free of suffering. Hallelujah.

> *I think I like it. It's always warm.*
> *I see the frost of winter, but never shiver.*
> *My hands are clean.*
> *The blood is gone.*
> *I don't run anymore.*
> *I'm never alone.*
> *I used to relive my death.*
> *Now I can't place it, and I stopped trying.*
> *It's far away from me.*

TWENTY-ONE

———

I had taken Patricia by the hand and led her into a beautiful place, one reserved for the clean and the pure who have been washed by the loving hands of the angels who await them. It was not a place for the living. I was privileged to have been able to accompany her there. Sometimes, the sight I was born with does have its rewards.

But—and this is a big but—I was still recovering from what I'd come to call the Acts of Patricia. I think it will take years to resolve all of the effects of her possession. She had shredded my bills, and I had to make good with numerous utility companies. She had thrown out one jury-duty questionnaire, which was better than what she did with the next one that arrived—she sent it back under her name and listed "city morgue" as her place of residence. That one was a hoot to clear up, let me tell you.

I had thought that freeing Patricia would force Eddie

and his devil twin back into the hole they had come from. But that wasn't what happened. The visits from the tall man in black continued, and they were more intense than ever. He had been forced to let Patricia go, and I now realized that he had turned that focus to me. He did not want to give me up, too.

Will and I talked about putting our home up for sale, just to get away from Eddie—and all the entities before him. It felt good to think we could start over. We'd done it before. So we tried again. I looked online at listings every night for five months. Every house I thought would fit us when I saw it on the computer would turn out to be, well, unsuitable when I saw it in person. The minute I set foot on the steps of the houses we looked at, I could tell there had been a murder there. The real estate agents would finally disclose it when I asked. It was the universe telling us that we couldn't get away that easily.

Will and I went to an open house. The real estate lady greeted us at the door, a cute gal in her midforties, well-suited for the job. I smiled at her but walked in without shaking her hand. I just didn't want to pick up anything— if I shook her hand, I'd know her whole life story, and I just needed a break. It was nothing personal. For goodness' sake, I pick up on things when I try clothes on in a department store—the thoughts of the last people who tried it on, maybe even the factory workers who sewed it. At this point, I needed to limit my exposure.

We walked through the house. I knew instantly that

Will wasn't interested in the place because it needed too much work. I wasn't interested either, because it was too small for me and my big old Southern furniture and art. There was no place for my ornate mirrors. Or my boxed-up demons.

I didn't want to leave too quickly and hurt the agent's feelings, though, so I went upstairs. The master bedroom was the last room on the left. I pushed the door open and got a very uneasy feeling, the kind I get when spirits are right next to me. I fought down the panic but didn't leave. I opened the closet door. It was full of clothes, packed to the ceiling. Not a good selling point, certainly. I stood and stared and slowly, the hangers began to move. Then I saw his eyes from behind the clothes. The hangers parted and he spoke.

"You can't hide, Jackie. You can't run or move. Not without me. I thought we made that clear."

I backed up, found Will, and hauled him past the shocked gaze of the real estate agent and out of that house. He asked if I was okay. Thankfully, with him I didn't have to explain beyond what I said. We can't leave our place yet, I told him. I knew what I had to do. I had to visit Eddie in prison. He had asked me to come see him, and I had to do it, as a last homage to Patricia and all his other victims—both known and unknown—and as the only way I knew of to free myself. The only way out was in.

I scheduled a date with the prison officials and began to prepare. It was hard to even think of all the time I lost as Jackie while Patricia was with me. Now, what would I lose as I faced her killer? How was I supposed to feel? What was it that he wanted to say face-to-face? I didn't want to see any clients in the days leading up to this meeting. I needed a quiet mind and all of my strength. My armor needed to be rock solid. I wanted to just creep up on him as he always did to me, as he did to all of his victims.

Many things crossed my mind. Having to sit there in front of him. Watching him smiling and laughing at the thought of his escape in the most unlikely way, via a woman. In me. He still hoped for this, I knew. And I feared that possibility. The demon who knew how to separate the soul from the body was waiting for me.

As the day came closer, I could not sleep. His energy filled my space. Family pictures I had on the walls moved around as I sat in bed and watched. The heavy smell of rotting meat was all around me. His dark outline stood right in front of my bathroom door. I would break into a sweat and could not slow my pounding heart as he watched me. I would close my eyes and ask for strength from my spirit guides, my medicine men and spiritual warrior ancestors, and one of my favorites, Saint Anthony. *Please, help me. Please, God, don't let him in!*

The phone would ring off the hook at all hours. I'd watch his number come up on the caller ID, but would not pick up. I could feel his frustration as he'd slam down the phone. He knew I was coming. And I knew I did not need his voice seeping into my head. Not now.

I did not speak to anyone for those few days before I left for the prison. It took the same form of preparation an exorcism does—bracing myself for a confrontation with the master of darkness. *Don't let anything in. Don't let your human side become weak with any personal conflict. Avoid arguments—they are a diversion. Don't stray off your path.*

My mother used to tell me that the devil could knock on your door in any shape or form he wished. I couldn't let Eddie escape. Sure, his body would wither away in solitary confinement, but if he got his way, he would complete the work of the Zodiac through me. The devil had been trying to beat down my door for my whole life. He wasn't going to finally get in via a serial killer sitting in a prison visiting room. I was going to use every device at my disposal.

A week before the scheduled visit, I went to Saint Patrick's Cathedral in New York City. I emptied my plastic water bottle into a beautiful plant outside the church and walked inside for Mass. I filled the bottle with holy water from a huge marble font and then waited my turn for Holy Communion. When it was finally my turn, I knelt down and folded my hands. The priest looked at me over his glasses and asked if I was ready. "Like never before," I whispered.

He placed the Body of Christ in my hand and made the sign of the cross. "God be with you," he said.

"I need it, Father," I replied.

I walked to a pew in the back and sat down. I slid the bottle out of my coat pocket, broke the wafer in half, and put both pieces inside. I put the cap back on and shook it. The Body of Christ dissolved and swirled like a snow globe. I thought of the equivalent of a psychic blizzard that was coming my way, and my worry increased. People next to me in the pew looked at me in puzzlement. "Oh, yeah, this! It's a long story . . ." I said. They nodded apprehensively and scooted farther away down the bench. I would have given me a wide berth, too.

The church emptied after Mass, but I stayed seated, asking God for guidance. The priest passed by me and asked if I was okay.

"Yes, Father, but could you bless me? Please."

He looked me in the eye. "I already did. You and that holy water bottle of yours."

"Father, I'm weak," I said.

He stood in the aisle of that great cathedral and looked at me as though he knew what I was going to do. Then he smiled. "No, you're not. Go, and God will not let you down."

He moved on down the aisle as images of my mother's failed exorcism crowded into my head. "He has before," I said as I got up and stood in the aisle as well. "No disrespect, Father, but I need help."

He turned back toward me and said, "I know God will not let you down. I am not an exorcist."

"How did you know? Father, please tell me!" I said.

"I know a lot," he said. "You aren't alone. You are blessed."

He walked off, and I took my blessing gratefully and fled. I had seen the devil in God's house before, and I didn't want to chance it again now.

I kept the bottle on my home altar until I left to go see Eddie. It sat alongside my father's and my granddaddy's medicine bags, pictures of my ancestors, a burning candle, the hair of the wolf, food offerings, and a handful of graveyard dirt for the dead—earth to earth.

Experts seem to believe that serial killers leave marks on their victims' bodies or leave items, like letters, nearby as their calling cards. Psychologists in this field will tell you that it is a cry to get caught, that the killers want to lead the police right to their doors. But in my dealings with these people, I can tell you this: they do not want to get caught. That's the last thing they want. They do what they do to defile the body further. They mark their territory and leave the task force something to chase but not enough to find them. They enjoy the torment. They enjoy giving you enough to ask a question but not enough to ever find the answer. Psychologists can only assume what makes the bomb tick. But until you *become* the bomb, you will never know.

I sought the answers and found out who Eddie really was. He knew that now and waited for me. We are all born of flesh, but something more settled into Eddie a long time ago. His mind and body guarded the demon with care, feeding it and keeping it safe from exposure. What nestled within was far more deadly than any man-made weapon. The things we chalk up to hysteria are the same things that build momentum for evil. People do not wish to believe, but awareness is actually the first, best weapon. And I was very, very aware of Eddie.

It would not be my first time standing before the devil,

THE HAUNTING OF THE GEMINI 257

of course. I have rejected his enticements, but never will I deny his existence. This was a test of my endurance and belief. I knew—have known for years—that I am marked. My face is on one of those old "Most Wanted" posters. I am wanted, not for committing crimes but for how I have solved them. The criminals know I'm out here. They know I am watching them as they watch me, seeing how far I get.

The four-hour drive to the Great Meadow Correctional Facility was exhausting. It was interstate the first part of the way but not a very heavily traveled one. Except for some tractor-trailers speeding by, we were alone on the road. I had asked my friend Maria Dinaso to come with me. She has worked closely with Joanne and me for many years. Not many people can handle the crime scenes or the paranormal activity, but she can. She's a strong woman, well trained by me and knowledgeable of other-worldly activity. I knew I couldn't make this drive by myself, and her steady presence was a comfort as we got closer and closer to Great Meadow. I didn't want Will or Joanne to come with me because I thought it would put them in spiritual danger to be so physically near Eddie. They were closer to me than Maria and so would make better targets for Eddie's manipulations.

Throughout the years, my mind has become so piercing that I've had to give up driving; every passing car is a distraction, because I hear the thoughts of everyone inside. It's become too overwhelming to try to tune that out and focus on the road at the same time, so I don't get behind the wheel anymore.

For instance, as we sped along, I saw a car on the side of the highway, an old maroon Chevy. As we drew closer, I fixated on it. I could see a young man wearing a brown ski hat inside the car, trying to fight his way out. He pounded on the windows and looked right at me, his face tearstained and panic stricken. I heard him shout, "Help me!" And then the Chevy burst into flames.

Maria hadn't seen anything. Neither had the big-rig driver who passed at the same time. But the young man's face of ash filled my whole field of vision. I felt it was another of Eddie's victims, reaching out to me in a vision prompted by my increasing proximity to him. Witnessing and not being able to help is unbelievably painful. Seeing the brutality of what Eddie had done was horrendous. I slumped in the passenger seat, and the miles crawled by.

We left the interstate and started down the two-lane highway that would lead us to the prison. I roused myself as I saw another young man, about twenty-five years old and holding a small cardboard sign, come into view on the side of the road. "Don't stop—don't pick up that hitchhiker," I told Maria. She looked at me and back at the winding road. "What hitchhiker?" she asked.

I studied him as we drove closer. I could now see that he was obviously dead. He had visible gunshot wounds to the head, which was dangling almost off his neck. His skin was blue and covered with old bloodstains. He wore torn jeans and a faded blue T-shirt. He had no shoes, and his feet were filthy. A small, tattered, dark-blue knapsack sat on the ground next to him. I asked Maria to slow down so I could take in everything he wanted to show me. I saw something on his foot that I initially thought was a note of some kind. But as we slowed to a crawl, the paper moved and I could read it: a tag stamped "NYC Morgue," along with the name "John Doe, 1993." I knew he had been homeless. His cardboard sign, in red writing, said "TURN BACK!"

Maria looked at me and asked if we should turn around, even though she couldn't see the man or his sign. I told her no. We had come too far—literally and figuratively. I needed to be on Eddie's ground, to look him in the eye.

The wind picked up, bending the trees and shoving the car all over the road. Maria hung on to the steering wheel and kept us in our lane. A big rig approached from the other direction. I stared at it and knew that the driver would become distracted. I kept looking as we sped toward each other. Suddenly, the driver reached down for something, taking his eyes off the road. I yelled for Maria to hit the gas. Our car shot forward just before the tractor-trailer crossed into our lane. We both looked at each other with the same holy-shit expression. Once she recovered her breath, Maria asked what I was thinking.

"Eddie is toying with us," I said.

"Yeah," she replied. "I have to agree. If he wanted us dead, he would have made sure of it."

We were about a half hour away when Maria needed a break. I didn't want to stop, but she had a point. She would be waiting in the car the entire time I was in the prison with no way to use a bathroom. So we pulled over at a run-down gas station. She went around the back to the restrooms while I stayed in the car, worrying about everyone at home. I hoped they were okay. Bad things seem to ricochet and come back at you from unexpected directions. Usually where it hurts the most. I checked my phone—no calls or texts. I hoped that meant no bad news.

I impatiently tossed my phone in the back and laid on the horn. What the hell was taking Maria so long? I was getting more and more antsy as we got nearer. I felt very alone already, and sitting by myself in a car in front of a dilapidated gas station was not helping. I was reaching for the horn again when Maria rounded the corner of the building, waving a piece of paper.

"Come on. What the hell are you doing?" I said. "We have a timeline."

She was talking away, but I couldn't make out what she was saying as she climbed into the car. She tossed the paper at me as she buckled up. It was a piece of construction paper with what looked like a child's drawing on it. A little girl held the hand of a woman who looked like me, complete with my shock of black hair. And the girl wore a yellow coat.

"What is this, Maria?" I managed to choke out.

"You tell me," she said.

She had heard a girl come into the bathroom while she was in the stall. It was a little creepy, Maria continued. The bathroom had no windows, was badly lit, and felt a little like a dungeon. When she came out to wash her hands, the girl was standing in the corner. Maria said she asked the girl if she was okay. The girl walked over and said, "Give this to her."

"Her who?" Maria asked.

"Who I am now," she said the girl replied, before handing Maria the drawing and running off.

"Not through the door," Maria told me as we sat in the car, "but through the wall." She turned to look at me. "Okay, now I'm losing my mind. Tell me I'm losing my mind, and I'll feel better."

I couldn't tell her that. Before I could come up with something else to say, she shook her head and rubbed her face, trying to shake it off. "Forget it," she said. "Who am I to think anything is strange?"

I silently folded the drawing and hid a smile. It was confirmation. Jane was still by my side. Maria asked again if I was sure I hadn't seen a girl in a yellow raincoat. I shook my head. I had never told her about the child I had been in a former life, and I did not have the strength to go into it right then.

We continued on and finally reached the prison. The parking lot was almost empty. The prison itself looked like a fort, with a thirty-foot wall surrounding it. There was little vegetation around, like even the soil itself was tainted in this place. And there to greet me were the dead. It was a line of souls, ghostly figures who had once lived and loved, who now seemed to be waiting for their chance to confront the people who took their last breaths. They showed the scars from their wounds and from their autopsies. Some had faces so torn apart I could not make them out. They stood in a line right up to the prison walls. I knew they wanted their own revenge, not against me but against those inside the prison, but I did fear them. Maybe they were waiting for me to lead them inside.

It is said that God comes in strange ways. But the devil does, too. He brings certain people together, and it is not mistake or coincidence. In the end, you have only your faith to carry you forward. And you can go forward, but you can't reach the castle until you defeat the monsters of the forest first.

I got out of the car with the drawing in my bag and walked through the gate. I did not look back.

TWENTY-TWO

———————

I stopped in the bathroom before I reached the guard station and pulled my water bottle out of my bag. The prison wives and girlfriends crowded in the bathroom with me. They took turns using a small mirror to doll themselves up. Everyone was chattering excitedly, and no one noticed me douse my head with my murky-looking liquid. Never underestimate your opponent. I said a prayer for my safe return as the holy water dripped down off my hair. It was time.

At the guard station, I gave the officer Eddie's name and ID number and handed over my own ID. It was like going through security at the airport. Belt off, clothing inspected, searched head-to-toe. The guard went through my bag and pulled out a box of crayons. An entire box of just the color red.

"Hey, you can't take this in," he said. "And how did you find a box of all red crayons? Is this a joke?"

I'd had no idea it was in there, and I had no idea where it had come from. I couldn't tell him that, though. I cleared my throat. "No, sir. It must have been my kid. The things they do. I will definitely have a talk with her when I get home. Silly little girls . . ." I rambled on for a minute, playing dumb. It was better than telling him the truth. He eyed me carefully and told me I could have them back after my visit. I smiled. Of course.

He was a hard-ass, but I didn't blame him. These correctional officers put their lives at risk every day as they dealt with the most deadly criminals around. One slipup can cost many lives. This hit home as he slid a paper toward me to sign that stated that if an incident should unfortunately occur, authority figures would not be held responsible for my life or safety. Basically, you're on your own. Well, I was certainly familiar with that. I signed it and went inside.

I passed through several checkpoints on my way to Eddie. It was like going on a road trip, where you tour faraway lands and show your papers at dusty outposts. With each one, I felt like I was farther and farther from American soil. By the time I got to the visiting room, I was definitely in a foreign land.

Other people filled the room, family members and friends of the incarcerated. As I watched them eagerly await their loved ones, I couldn't help but think about what the loved ones of all the victims were doing at that moment. All those families and friends of all those murder victims, all over the world. They didn't get visiting hours. They didn't get Christmas cards in the mail. They just got to go through life in a state of half existence. They just got to rattle around in a garden that once bloomed but was now choked with weeds. The loved ones of murder victims deserved more than that.

I was ushered to a seat at a small school-type desk, just like the one I'd seen so many times in Eddie's bedroom. Just like the one he sat and plotted at, as a child and as a man. And his terrible visions had come true.

A large gate banged open and the inmates filled the room, heading for their visitors. They all walked and dressed the same, but their one real element in common was internal. They had all found God. Their thoughts were so clear. "The burden is now in God's hands. See, I'm all better now that I'm locked up." Too bad they hadn't figured this out before they made the choices that brought them here. Still, it was ironic. The one thing most people on the outside had lost, they had found.

And then there was the last person to enter. Two armed guards came through the gate. One stopped and held it open, and then there Eddie stood, just as I have seen him so many times. In my home. In my dreams. In my bedroom. In my mirror. Beside me. Within me. And then, like the double exposure of a photo, there appeared to my eyes the tall man in black, right over Eddie, his twin.

The tall man in black dissolved, and again, it was just Eddie. He mouthed something silently, but I heard it from twenty feet away as though he were whispering in my ear.

"We are together again."

The visiting room turned quiet as a tomb. The guards stood still as mannequins. The chatter of others died away. Everyone began to fade. Eddie had that ability. As my eyes went slowly around the room, I saw him doing the same thing. He held his hands out, free from restraints, and smiled. Time began again, and the guards started to move forward. Both kept hands on their guns as they walked alongside him. He was the only prisoner who got such an escort, all the way to the little desk where I sat. We were kept away from the rest of the inmates and visitors, toward the back of the room. No one was sure of what Eddie would do.

As he approached, I noticed a huge clump of dust blow out from the corner and stop right at my foot. Eddie chuckled as he pulled out his tiny chair and then spoke before I could say a word.

"Isn't this cozy, Jackie? I like how you noticed the insignificant ball of dust. To them it all means nothing. Only you looked. Only you followed it with your eyes." He turned in his chair, taking in the entire room, where people were slowly returning to movement and talk. He turned back. "Let's talk about that ball of dust, Jackie."

I sat and watched him as he spoke. How could he get up every day knowing what he had done? But that slipped from my thoughts quickly, because I knew what drove him, the dark soul underneath that needed to be fed.

"It was a test, and you passed. The others passed, but

not the same way. They weren't supposed to notice. Just like the thousands of people that don't see or believe. You see. You noticed something that everyone else takes for granted. It means nothing; it had no meaning. No money, no future or past. But yet, it has substance and takes up space, so just because they didn't see it roll around the room, does it mean it doesn't exist?"

I knew what he was talking about. The things, the people, the actions that slip by other people. I looked into his eyes and saw the deep black pools, sharp and cunning, showing me the demon that dwelled in him. And that now sat across from me in the flesh.

He asked me how it had felt to witness the killings, the screams, the fires, the torture. How I couldn't do a damn thing about it. How I must live with it. How did it feel to be a victim? He grabbed my hand. "I'm sorry, Jackie, I couldn't wear black for you, the clothes you're used to seeing me in. They don't allow it in[side] these walls I creep in and out of." He closed his eyes and began quoting bastardized Bible verses. "And the Lord was my weak lamb; I shall fear not a fucking thing. Oh, how the flock is weak!" He smiled and caressed my hand. I took his hand off mine and put mine under the desk.

"Enough, Eddie. I'm not scared of you. I'm here now. What do you want from me?" I wanted him to back off, and I wanted to give myself time to figure out what he was up to.

He sat back and said, "I want to show you something pretty extraordinary."

We stared at each other and then I felt something

cutting into the palm of my right hand, fast and hard. I pulled my hands out from under the desk. There, plain as day, a series of letters was carved into my right hand, all with jagged edges that were starting to bleed.

My name is Patricia and you killed me!

I quickly squeezed it into a fist and covered it with my left hand. I didn't want the guards or superintendent to see and think I had smuggled in something. I had been terrified for weeks that Patricia would inhabit my body when I finally saw Eddie. But she wanted to face him. She was back because she wanted to show him that she was no longer scared. She had stopped running.

Eddie looked at me and said in an almost boyish tone, "Oh, come on, let's see what you got. Come on, Jackie, let's play peekaboo, just like in those disgusting peep shows."

The sweat started to run down my face. I put my hand forward and showed him the message. I suddenly smelled fear from him. His back stiffened. "How dare you, Jackie? Think you could outwit me by showing me what I have done? You're right, I didn't know her name. Nor did I care to."

I felt Patricia pushing me aside. I struggled frantically to get back in, terrified that I would be left outside, stuck here forever with Eddie. He could see this and watched us both. "Okay," he said to Patricia, "you got what you want."

"Why did you kill me?" The question exploded out of me.

Eddie crossed his legs. Frost came out of his mouth. "Is it cold in here, or is it the frigid temperature of that cold, steel, lonely place—the end of the end? Can you hear the door slam? The tight coffin lid? The sickening stench of your remains?" His eyes rolled back with lustful pleasure.

Patricia sat up a bit taller. "No, Eddie, I don't!" she hissed. "That doesn't exist in my world, not anymore. You're the one stuck in hell. In spirit, you're able to leave and roam, invading other people. But in flesh, in the reality of the human race, you are and will always be in a cage. You can only live through a host."

I pushed—so hard I almost fainted—and got her to step back. I grabbed his hand with mine and pressed the bloody message into his palm. He tried to pull away. "No, Eddie. You're going to relive your deranged life. Feel me, Eddie. See me now. It's Jackie, not your helpless victim and all the others. Look at your own mirror now. Look in my eyes."

We stared into each other's eyes. I hadn't planned on this when I arrived, but now I knew that I needed to take him back and show him the child that he was before the devil came to him. That was my plan, anyway.

I saw myself running up the staircase of an apartment building. Babies cried and people fought and screamed behind closed doors. Old, dusty liquor bottles littered the steps. Eddie was in me, and this was his home, the drug-infested projects. As I made my way up the stairs, I could feel the glee in him build. "I'm home, Mom!" *Not so fast, Eddie*, I thought. I held on to the stair railing with both hands, because I was starting to hear the screams.

If people had been watching us in the visiting room, all they would have seen were two people sitting very still and holding on to each other with a death grip. But inside, my grasp on that stair railing was slipping. I heard every scream come from every one of his victims. It wasn't a few, or even several. It was a crowd full of moans and pain tearing through as if it had broken free and was finally able to rip him apart. Just as he had done to them and their families.

I looked up, trying to find the ceiling of the prison visiting room—the real, concrete world. *With all that is good and pure, God, please help me.* My grandfather and more. All the souls I have helped find their ways back home. *Show mercy on me. Give me only strength.* But I stayed in the stinking tenement stairwell. Eddie kept pulling me toward his old apartment. I knew now that I would not find the child Eddie. There was nothing left of him but what the devil already owned. And I knew that if he succeeded at dragging me inside that apartment, which symbolized the devil's house and the graves of all his victims, I would never leave this real-world prison. He would become the keeper of my soul, and my body would leave these walls looking like Jackie but housing Eddie. He would walk free. To complete his deeds upon the human race. Through me. I would be the Zodiac Killer. The Gemini. The body of Jackie and the soul of Eddie.

In the tenement, one hand reached for the door knob. I heard an older woman say, "Eddie, is that you?" He wanted to say, "I'm home, Mommy," but I pressed my lips shut, muffling his voice and hopefully stopping his advance. He turned on me. "Open your fucking mouth and eat me," his voice roared in my head. "Take my body. We are one. Drink from my cup and spill the blood."

We were there now. His doorway was at my fingertips. I felt lifeless—heavy and dull and empty. Was this what it would feel like when that door opened? He pushed my hand toward the knob. And then the light appeared. A bright ball came through the building's roof as it cracked open. Debris fell past me and crashed down flights of stairs. The light tumbled with it, reaching the corners of horror. And out of it came a man with rolled-up sleeves and a top hat. He held the hand of little Jane, and his steps sounded like thunder. He brought her closer and her voice echoed through the dark hallways.

"Let her go! You have no power to kill anymore!" Jane turned toward me and pointed. "Run, Jackie. Come up toward the light."

I pulled myself up and heard the chants of an American Indian war dance. I felt the power flow into me like a blood transfusion. And I walked past Eddie's door. He screamed in rage and failure. And I kept walking.

Jane and her faithful Jacob moved aside and took the light with them. Behind it was a cinder-block cell with only a desk, a sink, and a hole for a toilet. This was Eddie's real home. I wrestled with him—I had to get him back into his dungeon. I looked behind me and saw that Jacob and Jane, in the yellow raincoat, had been replaced by Will and my Forever Guardian, the spirit of the eight-year-old Jackie who died on the operating table and had protected me ever since. I stared in thankfulness. Will had always been my protector. This showed me that he always would be. It gave me such strength and hope that I was able to turn back around and face the cell, which was clear as day in my vision.

Eddie sat at his tiny school desk humming a lullaby. "You will always bear the mark of the twin. You are everyone's twin." He leaped up and raced for the cell door. "You are the open gate to hell, like it or not."

I let go of Eddie's hand. The murmurs of other visitors drifted past. The guards still stood at their stations. I pulled my hand away and opened it, palm up. The writing was gone. He looked around the room in a panic. "You brought all my victims up with you! Didn't you, Jackie?"

I settled into my chair. "No. They came on their own to confront the person who cowardly killed them." He covered his eyes. I reached out and yanked his hands down, and he pushed back and out of his chair.

The guard rushed over, demanding, "Sit down, or I'll put you down."

Eddie squirmed under the authority and apologized. But I saw his eyes drift down to the guard's gun. He licked his lips. Always wanting the power.

The guard sat him back in his chair. I could still see the desire for the gun in his eyes. "Eddie, let go of the demon."

"No, never," he said. "It's what keeps me alive. And someday I shall be out. I will find you. You can't shake me off that easy, Jackie." He stared at me like he was gearing up for something. And, boy, was he.

"Oh, I saw your mother," he said. "All done up like a whore and—"

I stopped him. The idiot had no idea. "If you did, you wouldn't be alive to speak about it."

He scoffed at me. "The priest couldn't help her. God was too busy, Jackie. She was like you. Having this extra-special intelligence, this passage to the other side."

I started, "Eddie, this isn't about my mother—"

"Don't you call me mother. Wash your mouth out with poison, you little bitch," the voice of my mother came out of Eddie. It was one of many that came out of him during the hours I spent with him. He mimicked people I love, people I have lost—trying to break me so he could slide inside and then out the prison gates he would go.

"Now that we tested each other in person, in the flesh, what do you want me to say, Jackie?" he asked, back to being Eddie. "That I'm sorry?"

Now I was the one scoffing. I knew he would never apologize. He started touching on different subjects, and throughout it all, he did not blink once. Occasionally, he would close his eyes in pleasure or triumph, but that was it. I realized that you don't notice when a person blinks, but you sure notice when he doesn't. It was one more demon-tainted trait in a being full of them.

"Let's talk about us, Jackie," he said. "You know I can go into anyone I choose, any crack, and live through that person. But only you, the medium, can see me. There has to be a better name for your gift. It's extraordinary. I bet there must be a high price on your head, knowing the things you know. And it's how you deliver that makes you so fascinating.

"Look at these walls and watch the magic show begin," he demanded. "Look! Now don't cheat." I looked around the visiting room, from the ceiling on down. I saw people chatting, a guard chewing gum a few feet away. I glanced back at Eddie and saw him squeeze his eyes shut and hold his lips tight until saliva foamed from one corner. I knew what he was doing—causing a psychic illusion. *Here we go*, I thought.

Large cockroaches began to pour out of the seams in the ceiling. Thousands poured out until I couldn't even see the wall anymore. They engulfed the guard, covering his face, going into his mouth, sticking to his chewing gum, running up his shirtsleeves and down his collar and into his nose. The sound of their wings and legs rubbing filled my ears as they took over the entire room, going in and out of every human opening possible. And everyone acted as though nothing was wrong.

"Are you done?" I asked. I closed my eyes tightly and made my own psychic illusion of a large hole in the wall. It became a suction hose and pulled every last bug in before snapping shut.

"Very good, Jackie!" Eddie clapped his hands. He was already thinking of his next trick, though. He told me he could make the guard not see and then use the opportunity to snap my neck. He would make sure no one noticed until all the inmates were back in their cells. Then there would just be a dead woman and a prison guard in the room. The guard might go down for murder, he said gleefully. But a second later, his ego backed off that goal.

"But again, that would be my work," he said. "You don't think Michelangelo would let someone else take his work!"

And if I had learned anything, it was how proud Eddie was of his "work."

"Why do you think Patricia contacted me from the grave using your body?" he asked.

I sat and looked at him. "Why, Eddie? You tell me."

"Because I needed you to free me once and for all." He was trying to convince me that he had been in control of all this from the beginning. That he had been the one who sent Patricia to me so that he could get my attention and use me for his own ends. Bullshit. Patricia had found me on her own. Patricia had found her freedom, and I'd helped her. Eddie could sit there and rationalize all he wanted, but his victim had escaped him. He had no power over her anymore.

"And you took her away from me." He continued talking. "I kept her in prison—my prison—dying over and over again. Can you imagine reliving your death over and over again? Climbing those steps in that drug-infested park. Thinking I wanted to fuck her. I watched her struggle like a pig. The first few blows staggered her. Confusion, disoriented, bleeding. The shock across her face.

"It was like a young boy catching Santa Claus coming down the chimney covered in snow and frost, shaking bells and unloading his sack of bodies—I mean goodies—

for all the little boys and girls . . ." Sometimes his tangents made very little sense. "Anyway, I was so thrilled to watch her. When I had enough of her fighting to get up, I stabbed her. The more I plunged the blade, the blood would come up at me like striking oil! Squirt! Squirt!

"You know the amazing thing—I didn't have any blood on me. I couldn't figure it out. Sure, a little on my hands . . . I walked away. Not run, walked. My master covered me. Oh boy, was I going to take down so many.

"Sure, I wanted my prisoner back. I used to stick my finger in the bullet holes and dig around while she moaned. I needed some entertainment. And you took her away." He glared at me. "You know the Bible says 'An eye for an eye.'"

I met his gaze. "Yeah, Eddie. It does. It also says 'And thou shalt not kill.'"

He laughed. "Good one, Jackie." Because, to him, that was a joke.

TWENTY-THREE

———◆———

Crime writers, newspapers, television—they all paid
too much attention to the victims, he said. I stared at him.
What the hell was he talking about? They were the
victims.

"Exactly!" he said. "Only when the person is killed do
others have sympathy. Where were they when she was
roaming the streets? And strapped down in restraints in
those mental institutions? Selling her body? I only ask for
the truth to come out. We all see the descent, but no one
speaks about it. Let's just hint around. I'm not saying she
is less a victim. But why does everyone care after the fact?
Ask yourself that."

He had a point on this one. Most people don't care
when these lost people are alive, when they can still be
helped, when they can still be saved. It's a lot easier
to pretend they are not there. That is where we as a

society fail. We lock up the killers, but we don't care for their victims before it's too late.

He eyed me. "Okay, Jackie, what is the question you're holding back?"

In some of our numerous telephone conversations, he had eluded to actions or phrased sentences in a way—like referring to people as dessert—that made me think he had done something unspeakable.

"Did you ever cannibalize anyone?" I asked.

"Oh, I hate that word. It seems so animalistic," he said. "Does licking a bloody knife fall under that? The flesh is much too tough. And how would I cook them with Mom in the house?"

He paused and looked at me.

"I have my ways, Jackie. Ask yourself this. Where did all the blood go? Let's look at our friend Patricia. One hundred gaping wounds and gunshots, and the pigs thought she overdosed?"

I thought about Patricia, so cruelly forgotten by society, and then so cruelly used by Eddie. I looked in his unblinking eyes and knew he was scoffing at my compassion.

"Getting into my mind is dangerous, Jackie," he said. "But we can't stop that. You were meant to catch the stars that fall from the blacked sky, the souls of others before being damned to hell. We are both on the same road, you on one side, me on the other.

"Is your cross heavy, Jackie? I see the pain in your eyes.

Put it down, hand it to me—that bag you wear around your neck. Pull it off and throw it in the sewer. Denounce your faith."

I was not wearing my mojo bag, with its amulets, herbs, and hair of the great wolf and of my father—it never would have made it past the security screening—but I knew what he meant. He wanted me to cast off all of my beliefs, my ancestral protection, my best defenses against the devil. Yeah, right. I wasn't stupid. "I couldn't wear it into the prison," was all I said. I wanted to see where he would take this line of talk.

"You know you don't have to," he said. "You embed it in your flesh. I smell it on you." Yet he really thought I might give it up?

"Not a chance in hell, Eddie," I said. "Your god may want me, but my God holds my hand."

He smiled. "Why be tormented your whole life? Your mother, Mary, didn't win."

"Yeah," I replied, "but I'm not her."

"Jackie, did anyone ever tell you Satan loves you? Your eyes are mirrors, holding the image of the suffering, the dead. Blue as the sky, oh, you do shine."

Eddie had already told me several times about how he'd loved to break into houses and spy on people. What was he thinking as he did that?

"That unsuspecting moment is so thrilling," he said, leaning in and licking his lips. "Now, don't ask anything yet, Jackie. Let's not get ahead of ourself [*sic*]. I want you to feel what it's like—not that you haven't, but why spoil the fun now? Begin to paint the picture in your oh-so-amazing mind . . . and feel the sheer panic when I was spotted sitting quietly in a chair, right in the next room.

"I didn't want to run right away. I wanted to see her flee . . . I didn't know her name, nor did I care to. But I feel her heart in my hands. Not a feeling like that in the world . . . I see her heart beat so fast her blouse was moving . . . her eyes popping out of her head . . . Her breathing was so heavy I could taste her breath, that gasp of air that struggles to come out." People think you scream in a situation like that, but you don't, he said. The mind can't accept it and the reflexes don't act quickly enough.

During one break-in, a woman about twenty-five years old came out of the bathroom to find the Zodiac Killer in her room. All these years later, the memory still makes him smile. "It looked like she saw a fucking ghost." She ran out and told her parents, who were in another part of the house. They called 911, and the operator asked who was in the house. The woman said she didn't know. "She looks back as I stand, looking directly at her, giving her time to take in every feature. Make no mistakes, I didn't run all the time . . . I come closer, out of the shadow and there in the flesh I stand. In that one moment, just one moment, I become a legend. And she knows in her heart and soul, the Zodiac lives."

He had apparently saved up his dramatic flair for me. He was definitely on a roll now.

"I turn and slip out the same way I got in, through a

very tiny crack. We both know those cracks, Jackie." He explained how he'd exited out the back, jumped a fence, and come walking out onto the main street about forty feet away. He heard the woman give the arriving cops a description of a large black man. The police even stopped and asked Eddie if he'd seen anyone with those features while he was standing on the street. "Why didn't she see me for who I am? Thank you, my master, for blinding the weak sheep."

Eddie loved that part, too. Hanging out at his own crime scenes. "Not so much to watch the excitement— cops throwing their hands up, the frustration on their faces, the hustle of going nowhere fast. I was learning my power over others. The best way to move was right along-side of you. The best way to hide is right in sight."

"Eddie, what do you do all day to occupy your mind?" I knew, of course, that he enjoyed torturing me psychi-cally, but I did wonder what else he did to fill his time.

He's housed in isolation and even eats alone. Breakfast is cereal in a cup passed through a slot in the door, and maybe an apple. That's at 5:00 a.m. Lunch is at 11:00, and is bologna and plastic-tasting cheese between two slices of bread. Dinner is at 3:00 p.m., and he gets two slices of bologna and some shredded lettuce. Once in a while, he'll get a grilled-cheese sandwich, and on holidays, a cookie. They won't give him a prison job, because they don't trust him. He insists he's too fearsome for anyone to come near him, for anyone to violate him like others are in prison all the time. He reads anything that has to do with war, murders, weapons, or history. He's allowed one preselected movie a month, but he only watches it if it matches those interests. He reads the Bible but twists it to accommodate the devil. He said he isn't allowed to attend the prison church. The man of the cloth will stop by his cell for a quick visit and hand him the yearly calendar, then flee.

"The church claims to help people in need," he said. "I went because I was killing. Something was inside me, forcing me, driving me. I was only the passenger at that time . . . I went to the church and spoke, telling the priest something was inside, taking over, and soon it will be too late."

He said he felt like he was the rot in the walls, covered with dry wall and plaster and pretty paint. But punch a hole through those layers, and they would have found him.

"I tried to get away from this, whatever this was. I took the test for the army. I failed by two lousy points. Two points—can you believe this? There were guys with visible track marks on their arms, sweating bad . . . I hated them. You could smell the fiends a mile away. Even the piss on them, it seeps through their pores. *They* got accepted. It was obvious I was being stopped."

I kept listening, the little desk chair hard against my back.

"It came to me—this thing, a dark figure—when I was very young, and detached from family. Alone. I was a good candidate. I was already isolated, I guess, not really loved. I'm not making excuses."

He kept on, talking about different things and then coming around again to religion.

"I'm just telling you the church is full of shit . . . They come by the prison to spread the word of pure bullshit. I can hear his thoughts as he walks by my cinder-block cage, doing his sign of the cross. Such lies. Hands me a calendar, of all things. The time I took from others, and the time I seem to have plenty of." He contemplated this for a moment, then continued. "His thoughts . . . 'I can't wait to get out of this place, grab a beer and a sandwich.' Father, I know what you're thinking! He runs past fast. I call out, 'I have sinned, Father, in the most unforgivable way. But so have you. I don't hide behind a cross. You do, Father. Satan didn't pound those nails in, Father. Man did!' He took off like a little girl."

The chair started to hurt, but I stayed still.

"Jackie, I have so much time. The devil won't let me die. I'm not getting soft, just stating a fact. Look at me. I haven't aged," he laughed.

He was right. He hadn't visibly aged at all. Compared with photos I'd seen of him from his court appearances in the 1990s, he looked just as good, if not better now. I stared at those black eyes, which bored into me. "Jackie, do you realize with your gifts what you could have done?" I did not respond. He told me to look at my hand, the one Patricia had scratched earlier. I unfurled my fist and saw now the sign of the Gemini, red and welted like a hot branding.

"You will always carry me with you," he said. "But the challenge will be—can you stop the evil . . . hold it down?

It will come to you always in the form of a sign. Oh, do you have your work cut out. Angels and demons aren't that far apart. We are the chosen ones."

I looked at my hand and closed my fingers tightly over the sign of my haunting.

"We are the same, Jackie. We fight for the same thing. I want it to be known that evil is pure and exists. And you fight to take it out of people. So we both know the truth.

"And yes, I'm a killer. I don't care about humanity. I don't feel bad for the body count—maybe a little because my plans got messed up. The devil Abaddon got mad, and, well, here I am. I don't care about the world. I don't care about time. I don't care about going before a parole board. I don't care about the families. I don't regret a fucking thing."

He talked faster and faster. "I do care about what weapons can cause the most damage—how many people can be taken down at once. I do like to watch the news, all the horrible things . . . I'm the man you tell your children about . . . I'm the night . . . If the world knew what you now know, I don't think they would go out after dark . . . I like to read about the occult, because it's as real as the nose on your face—as real as that New York City morgue, as that insane asylum. As real as over one hundred stab wounds and some shots . . . I like looking at symbols and signs on a dollar bill . . . I like candy." He took a breath and smiled. "I like you."

I kept my hand in a fist. Why, I asked, did he want me to tell the public about him—about his many unknown killings, about how he kept Patricia's spirit hostage, about how he can move from person to person?

"It's simple, Jackie. You are my confessional booth. You know what's in my mind and body. The world should know the truth. And only you can see past the mirror into the world that waits—good and bad. You see it all. You are the twin, a victim of murder that came back and slowly remembered. Remember, nothing is by chance."

"Are you scared, Eddie?"

"No, I'm scared of nothing. I know what lies past this life. And I know how to come back, just like you."

After the police arrested Eddie, someone wrote a true-crime book about him and the crimes they knew of at the time. This was also funny to him, even all these years later.

"He spoke to my mother. Gave her a few bucks to go in my room and interview her. She needed the money; I don't blame her. But if my own mother didn't know me, what could she tell him? . . . Don't make me laugh. So you show pictures of my room? Big shit."

He stared at me with those unblinking eyes. "Now, if you let me into your head and write who and what I really am and all the many things I've done . . . if you're able to hold my soul as you did, Jackie, now you got a fucking story to rock the hand of death . . . Live with me a few years, even a week, and you got a story no man has."

That author never sat down with him, Eddie said.

"You had the balls, Jackie—to not just sit with me but

listen for years about the faces of evil that I evolved into.
You let me into your head, your safe place, to solve the
puzzle. Big-shot detectives became tortured and obsessed
chasing that dragon but were scared to confront me. They
go by [the] textbook. You go by foot. You became me to
see exactly what I have done."

He leaned in. "You did something else, too. You
unlocked the past . . . and freed the damned. Doing so,
you found out who we both are. Yes, Jackie, I killed you
once upon a time. When you wore a yellow raincoat."

TWENTY-FOUR

I never wore the color yellow. It always hurt my eyes and affected my vision. And I never knew why. I always felt very protective of children, any children, and would go out of my way to help anonymously. When I worked with families victimized by crime, I would help them grieve by listening to their stories, their dreams, their heartbreaks. So many times, I would slip without realizing it and refer to myself as a victim of homicide. I would see flashes of a child who looked like me, but I did not then understand who she was or why she came to me. I would stop and have to compose myself in front of my clients. I was essentially holding my own hand through these sessions.

Even though I believe in reincarnation, for many years I could not bring myself to face my own previous death. And when I finally did, at first the anger grew. Someone took my life. Someone took my parents' world and burnt it down to the ground. I relived the pain of my death. But now I can see through the anger and the pain, and I realize that I am fortunate to know—it has allowed me to put down my heavy burden.

Jane helped show me heaven. She held my hand and reminded me how to experience only joy. It was not a word. It was a feeling, a touch, a sight like never before. I finally understood my journey, my life's purpose. I now know that my work isn't something that just left me in isolation from regular humanity. It was there to bring me to my own grave and then take me to a higher level. There was a purpose—not only for those I help but for me as well. I am truly blessed.

Eddie leaned forward slightly across the prison desk. "I didn't realize in the beginning of all of this that the devil was credited. Not until I saw myself change. Something is inside of me. It was a process. I welcomed it. I [have] thought about killing myself many times. And it stops me," Eddie said. "I don't care what people think. I have no interest in bullshit. I don't want fan mail. Such small minds," he laughed. "You once asked me, Jackie, if I met that girl in a dark street or down an alley, what would I do? I was quiet, Jackie, so you could feel my answer. I would take her face off in less than a minute."

Eddie in person was certainly honest, even more so than during our phone conversations.

"I'm no fucking joke. I'm not the one anyone wants to befriend."

"Eddie, what do you want the world to know?"

He thought for a moment, although there was still no blinking.

"I'm not the only one. My family didn't do this. The lack of food or money didn't. The proof is in my hands. I made those weapons with knowledge I didn't have. The lack of money didn't stop me. I wouldn't have it any other way. I accepted the devil long before I knew what was happening." And the devil, that tall man in black, had been with him ever since.

"People blame everything on poverty. I have no sense of guilt. Call me a sociopath; I don't care. But how many would wear my mask? How many have walked down dark alleys to hear my footsteps behind them?"

I tossed another question at him.

"Did anyone ever mention an exorcism to you?"

He sat back in his chair, and his eyes went completely black. The lights began to flicker. "I didn't think you would open such a can of worms in this lovely visiting room, with everyone at risk." This was obviously not a subject he wanted to address, so of course, I pushed him even more. He tried to change the subject, but I eventually steered it back around.

"Kill me, rid me of my pain." The voice that came from him was not his own. His eyes turned pleading and he grabbed my hand. "Don't let me linger. Save my soul . . ."

Then another voice, the one I was used to hearing from him, came forth in a vicious sneer. "Your soul? What soul?"

I pulled his hand off mine. "Why didn't those priests

that tried to help you—the ones that came up to the prison and the ones you went to see—"

He interrupted me. "They couldn't handle it. They came up and knew I needed help. Leaving was them telling the devil it won." He leaned over and clutched at his stomach in pain.

"Did they ever come back?" I asked.

"No, never," he said. "They came up in the beginning to Rikers Island and saw with their own eyes what was in me. They prayed over me and stopped. Just stopped and said among themselves—how could such a Bible-carrying man do such things? They questioned God! And they never, ever came back."

Before my visit, I'd gone to the church Eddie had frequented during the years he was committing all of his crimes. And I was turned away at the door. I told the priest that I was there for Heriberto Seda, and he bowed his head and shook it. "I can't," he said. "I'm not in good health." His faith was weak and fear ran through his blood. He knew what he would face if he allowed me to enter. So he asked me to leave. "God be with you. And all the angels," he said as he did the sign of the cross. "Go now."

It had been three hours since I first sat across from Eddie. I watched the clock the entire time, but he didn't look at it once. We had talked about many things, and I knew that he had not accepted that I would never be his escape hatch. That I would never do the devil's bidding. On the other hand, *I* knew now that I would never succumb to him. *I* realized that despite his terrorizing me, he would not win.

He picked his hand up off the table and held it out. "Bring your face to mine." I heard the snort of an animal come from him, low but distinct, when I didn't move toward him. "Are you afraid I will bite your face off?"

"No, Eddie, I'm not." I leaned forward until I was an inch away from him. "Do it, Eddie. Do what your gut tells you."

He touched my hair. He touched the holy water. The pain shot through his body like a bullet from a gun—I could feel it in him. His fingertips burnt. I could smell it.

"You tricked me, Jackie," he said. He started to slide his chair back, and I grabbed his arm to keep him in place.

"It's not me who commands you," I said. "It's God who commands you. Release this soul; depart to hell." I guess I never really give up hope that someone can be saved. Maybe someday, the devil will be forced out of Eddie. But not today. As I sat there, his face changed. The whites of his eyes disappeared, his breath turned foul and his skin wet and gray. I could smell the old blood on him. We locked hands.

"No, Jackie," he said. "It was your mother who condemned you to face evil. You will be haunted for the rest of your life."

Evil can enter anyone's life, but for him, I now realized that all the elements were in place long ago. The spotlight was on him, the people were fascinated and fearful, and he became a star. He liked that very much, even now.

The bell rang at that moment, just as he looked up at the clock. "Time's up," Eddie said. "Time, Jackie. You like that song." I did. "Time Is on My Side," by The Rolling Stones, has been my ring tone for more than six years, not that I'd ever told him that. He stood up, and the guards rushed over. "Is time on anyone's side?" he said. I did not answer, just moved to the edge of the room and waited for the iron gates to open so I could leave. The guards escorted him out the opposite side. "It's the Gemini," he said loudly. "The twin of the other." The door swung shut and he was gone.

EPILOGUE

Eddie tells me he can't hear Patricia scream anymore. She has found freedom, and so he has lost his hold on her. And he is taking it hard. He used to close his eyes at night, put his hand on his chest, and listen to her. It was her screams that would sing him to sleep.

And there were others in his walls, too. He was especially fond of the dog, that little white thing whose master he had shot and wounded all those years ago. The terrified barks and cries of the dog were also music to his ears. But now that is gone as well.

When they first faded away, Eddie searched his cell. He took the pictures off his walls and put his ear as close as he could. He listened high and low and couldn't hear a thing. This is very upsetting to him. It's as if he's lost an inner power that had kept him strong.

"Now they're gone, and I don't want to be here anymore," he said.

He has decided he needs to move on. Change the scenery. So, he told me, he's put in a request to transfer prisons. I don't know if that will happen. But I do know that all it would do is move the devil from place to place. There is nowhere to hide.

But as for me, my running has stopped. I still walk through the city and wonder how many demons walk among us and who they've targeted. But I now know that, even if they target me directly, I have the strength to take them on and beat them. After finally freeing Patricia and facing my own past life and death, I am more sure of who I am than ever before. I am a psychic medium, and I fight the devil.

My name is Jackie.